DOMESDAY BOOK

Huntingdonshire

History from the Sources

DOMESDAY BOOK

A Survey of the Counties of England

LIBER DE WINTONIA

Compiled by direction of

KING WILLIAM I

Winchester
1086

DOMESDAY BOOK

text and translation edited by

JOHN MORRIS

19

Huntingdonshire

edited from a draft translation prepared by

Sally Harvey

PHILLIMORE
Chichester
1975

1975

Published by

PHILLIMORE & CO. LTD.,
London and Chichester

Head Office: Shopwyke Hall,
Chichester, Sussex, England

© John Morris, 1975

ISBN 0 85033 130 7

Printed in Great Britain by
Titus Wilson & Son Ltd.,
Kendal

HUNTINGDONSHIRE

History from the Sources
General Editor: John Morris

The series aims to publish history
written directly from the sources
for all interested readers, specialists
and others. The first priority is to
publish important texts which should
be widely available, but are not.

DOMESDAY BOOK

The contents, with the folio on which each county begins, are:

Domesday Book is termed *Liber de Wintonia* (The Book of Winchester) in column 332c

INTRODUCTION

The Domesday Survey

In 1066 Duke William of Normandy conquered England. He was crowned King, and most of the lands of the English nobility were soon granted to his followers. Domesday Book was compiled 20 years later. The Saxon Chronicle records that in 1085

> at Gloucester at midwinter ... the King had deep speech with his counsellors ... and sent men all over England to each shire ... to find out ... what or how much each landholder held ... in land and livestock, and what it was worth ... The returns were brought to him.[1]

William was thorough. One of his Counsellors reports that he also sent a second set of Commissioners 'to shires they did not know, where they were themselves unknown, to check their predecessors' survey, and report culprits to the King.[2]

The information was collected at Winchester, corrected, abridged, chiefly by omission of livestock and the 1066 population, and fair-copied by one writer into a single volume. Norfolk, Suffolk and Essex were copied, by several writers, into a second volume, unabridged, which states that 'the Survey was made in 1086'. The surveys of Durham and Northumberland, and of several towns, including London, were not transcribed, and most of Cumberland and Westmorland, not yet in England, was not surveyed. The whole undertaking was completed at speed, in less than 12 months, though the fair-copying of the main volume may have taken a little longer. Both volumes are now preserved at the Public Record Office. Some versions of regional returns also survive. One of them, from Ely Abbey,[3] copies out the Commissioners' brief. They were to ask

> The name of the place; Who held it, before 1066, and now? How many *hides*?[4]
> How many ploughs, both those in lordship and the men's?
> How many villagers, cottagers and slaves, how many free men and Freemen?[5]
> How much woodland, meadow and pasture? How many mills and fishponds?
> How much has been added or taken away? What the total value was and is?
> How much each free man or Freeman had or has? All threefold, before 1066,
>   when King William gave it, and now; and if more can be had than at present?

The Ely volume also describes the procedure. The Commissioners took evidence on oath 'from the Sheriff; from all the barons and their Frenchmen; and from the whole Hundred, the priests, the reeves and six villagers from each village'. It also names four Frenchmen and four Englishmen from each Hundred, who were sworn to verify the detail.

The King wanted to know what he had, and who held it. The Commissioners therefore listed lands in dispute, for Domesday Book was not only a tax-assessment. To the King's grandson, Bishop Henry of Winchester, its purpose was that every 'man should know his right and not

---

[1] Before he left England for the last time, late in 1086.
[2] Robert Losinga, Bishop of Hereford 1079-1095 (see *E.H.R.* 22, 1907, 74).
[3] *Inquisitio Eliensis*, folio 1a.
[4] A land unit.
[5] *Quot liberi homines? Quot sochemani?*

usurp another's'; and because it was the final authoritative register of rightful possession 'the natives called it Domesday Book, by analogy from the Day of Judgement'; that was why it was carefully arranged by Counties, and by landholders within Counties, 'numbered consecutively ... for easy reference'.[6]

Domesday Book describes Old English society under new management, in minute statistical detail. Foreign lords had taken over, but little else had yet changed. The chief landholders and those who held from them are named, and the rest of the population was counted. Most of them lived in villages, whose houses might be clustered together, or dispersed among their fields. Villages were grouped in administrative districts called Hundreds, which formed regions within Shires, or Counties, which survive today with minor boundary changes; the recent deformation of some ancient county identities is here disregarded, as are various short-lived modern changes. The local assemblies, though overshadowed by lords great and small, gave men a voice, which the Commissioners heeded. Very many holdings were described by the Norman term *manerium* (manor), greatly varied in size and structure from tiny farmsteads to vast holdings; and many lords exercised their own jurisdiction and other rights, termed *soca*, whose meaning still eludes exact definition.

The survey was unmatched in Europe for many centuries, the product of a sophisticated and experienced English administration, fully exploited by the Conqueror's commanding energy. But its unique assemblage of facts and figures has been hard to study, because the text has not been easily available, and abounds in technicalities. Investigation has therefore been chiefly confined to specialists; a wide range of questions cannot be tackled adequately without a cheap text and uniform translation available to a wider range of students, including local historians.

Previous Editions
The text of the two volumes has been printed once, in 1783 by Abraham Farley, in an edition of 1,250 copies, at Government cost, originally estimated at £18,000 exclusive of salaries. Its preparation took 16 years. It was set in a specially designed type, destroyed by fire in 1808, here reproduced from the original edition. In 1816 the Records Commissioners added two more volumes, edited by Sir Henry Ellis, of introduction, indices, and associated text; and in 1861-1863 the Ordnance Survey issued zincograph facsimiles of the whole. Separate texts of many counties have appeared since 1673 and separate translations in the Victoria County Histories and elsewhere.

This Edition
Farley's text is used, because of its excellence, and because any worthy alternative would prove astronomically expensive. His text has been checked against the facsimile, and discrepancies observed have been

[6] *Dialogue de Scaccario*, 1, 16.

verified against the manuscript, by the kindness of Miss Daphne Gifford of the Public Record Office. Farley's few errors are indicated in the notes.

The editor is responsible for the translation and lay-out. It aims at what the compiler would have written if his language had been modern English; though no translation can be exact, for even a simple word like 'free' nowadays means freedom from different restrictions. Bishop Henry emphasized that his grandfather preferred 'ordinary words'; the nearest ordinary modern English is therefore chosen whenever possible. Words that are now obsolete, or have changed their meaning, are avoided, but measurements have to be transliterated, since their extent is often unknown or arguable, and varied regionally. The terse inventory form of the original has been retained, as have the ambiguities of the Latin.

Modern English commands two main devices unknown to 11th-century Latin: standardised punctuation and paragraphs. Latin *ibi* (there are) is usually rendered by a full stop, Latin *et* (and) by a comma or semi-colon. The entries normally answer the Commissioners' questions, arranged in five main groups, (i) the place and its holder, its hides, ploughs and lordship; (ii) people; (iii) resources; (iv) value; and (v) additional notes. These groups are usually given as separate paragraphs.

King William numbered chapters 'for easy reference', and sections within chapters are commonly marked, usually by initial capitals, often edged in red. They are here numbered, for ease of reference only. Maps, indices and an explanation of technical terms are also given. Later, it is hoped to publish full analytical tables, an explanatory volume, and associated texts.

The editor is deeply indebted to the advice of many scholars, too numerous to name, and especially to the Public Record Office, and to the publisher's patience. The draft translations are the work of a team; they have been co-ordinated and corrected by the editor, and each has been checked by several people. It is therefore hoped that mistakes may be fewer than in versions published by single fallible individuals. But it would be Utopian to hope that the translation is altogether free from error; the editor would therefore like to be informed of mistakes observed.

Huntingdonshire, Middlesex and Surrey have been the experimental counties at all stages of this edition. They may therefore contain more ineptitudes and mistakes than other counties.

The texts have been set by Sheila Brookshire, Jill Doig, Yvonne Grant, Auriol Hyde Parker, Isobel Thompson and Elizabeth Thorneycroft. The map is the work of Jim Hardy.

Conventions

*	refers to a note.
[ ]	enclose words omitted in the MS.
( )	enclose editorial explanations.

HVNTEDSCIRE.

IN BVRGO HVNTEDONE. Svɴ̃ . IIII . FERLINGI.
In duobʒ Ferlingis T.R.E. fuer̃ 7 funt m̃ . cxvi.
burgenfes c̃fuetudines om̃s 7 geldũ regis redden
tes. 7 fub eis funt . c . bordarij qui adjuuaɴ̃ eos ad
pſolutionẽ geldi . De his burgenfibʒ habuit Sc̃s
Benedict̃ de ramefy̆g . x . cũ faca 7 foca 7 om̃i c̃fue
tudine. tañtmodo gĩdabant T.R.E. Hos abſtulit
Euſtachius p uim de abbatia. 7 fuɴ̃ m̃ cũ ceteris
in manu regis.

Vlf fenifc ħƀ . xviii . burgenfes. m̃ hr̃ Giſleƀt̃
de gand cũ faca 7 foca . p̃ter gld̃ regis.

Aƀƀ de Ely̆ hr̃ . i . toftã cũ faca 7 foca . p̃t gld̃ r̃egis.

Ep̃s Lincolienfis ħƀ in Loco caſtri . i . manfionẽ
cũ faca 7 foca. quæ m̃ abeſt.

Siuuard̃ com̃ ħƀ . i . manfion̄ cũ domo cũ faca 7 foca
q̃etã ab om̃i c̃fuetudine . quã m̃ hr̃ Judita comitiffa.

In Loco caſtri fuer̃ . xx . manfiones ad om̃s c̃fue
tudines. reddentes p annũ . xvi . fol 7 viii . den̄ ad
firmã regis . quæ m̃ abfunt.

Præt̃ has fuer̃ 7 funt. lx . manfiones waſtæ
infra has ferling. quæ dabaɴ̃ 7 dant c̃fuetud fuas.

Et p̃ter has funt. viii . manfiones waſtæ . quæ
T.R.E. fuer̃ plenariæ. 7 dabant om̃s c̃fuetudines.

B In the Borough of HUNTINGDON

1 there are four quarters. In two quarters there were 116 burgesses before 1066, and still are. They pay all customary dues and the King's tax. Under them are 100 smallholders who aid them in discharging the tax. St. Benedict's of Ramsey had 10 of these burgesses with full jurisdiction and all customary dues, but they only paid tax before 1066. Eustace took them from the Abbey by force, and they are now in the King's hands, with the others.

2 Ulf Fenman* had 18 burgesses. Now Gilbert of Ghent has them, with full jurisdiction, apart from the King's tax.

3 The Abbot of Ely has one plot, with full jurisdiction, apart from the King's tax.

4 The Bishop of Lincoln had one residence, on the castle site, with full jurisdiction. It is not there now.

5 Earl Siward had one residence with a house, with full jurisdiction, exempt from all customary dues. Now Countess Judith has it.

6 On the castle site there were 20 residences liable for all customary dues, which paid 16s 8d a year to the King's revenue. They are not there now.

7 Besides these there were and are 60 unoccupied residences within these quarters* which gave and give customary dues.

8 Besides these there are also 8 unoccupied residences which were occupied before 1066 and gave all customary dues.

In alijs duobȝ ferlingis fueꝛ 7 funt cxl . burgenſ
diīn dom min . ad oīns c̄ſuetud 7 ad glđ regis.
7 iſti haƀ q̅t . xx . hagas ꝓ quibȝ dabant 7 dant
oīns c̄ſuetudines . De his ħƀ S̄ Benedict de Rameſy̆
xxii . burgenſ . T.R.E . Duo ex his fueꝛ đeti oīnibȝ
c̄ſuetud . 7 xxx . redđideꝛ quiſꝗ x . dẽn ꝑ annū.
Aliæ oīns c̄ſuetudines fueꝛ abƀis p̄t glđ regis.
In his ferling ħƀ Aluric T.R.E . uñ manſ . quā . W.
rex poſtea c̄ceſſit uxori ej 7 filiis . Euſtachi m̊ hꝝ.
quā paup cū matre reclamat . In his . ii . ferling
fueꝛ 7 funt waſtæ . xliiii . manſ . quæ dabaɴ 7 dant
c̄ſuetud ſuas . Et p̄ter has in his . ii . ferling habueꝛ
Borred 7 Turchil . T.R.E . i . æcclam cū . ii . hid terræ.
7 xxii . burg cū domibȝ ꝑtinent ad eand æcclam cū
ſaca 7 ſoca . quæ oīna hꝝ m̊ Euſtachi . Vnde ipſi reclamaɴ
miſcđam regis . Attaīn ipſi . xxii . burg daɴ regi oīnem
c̄ſuetud . Goiſfrid ep̄s hꝝ . i . æcclam 7 i . domū de ſuꝑ
dictis q̊s abſtulit S̄ Benedicto Euſtachi . 7 adhuc recla
mat iſđē Sc̄s . In ipſo burgo ħƀr Gos 7 Hunef . xvi . dom̊
T.R.E . cū ſaca 7 ſoca 7 thol 7 Them . Has hꝝ m̊ Judita

203 b

HVNTEDVN Burg defendebat ſe ad glđ regis
ꝑ quarta parte de Hy̆rſtingeſtan hund ꝓ . l . hid.
ſed m̊ non geldat ita in illo hund . poſtꝗ rex . W.
geldū monete poſuit in burgo . De toto hoc burgo
exibat T.R.E . de Landgable . x . liƀ . inde comes
tciā parte habebat . rex duas . De hoc cenſu reman
nc̄ ſuꝑ . xx . manſ ubi caſtrū . ē . xvi . ſol 7 viii . denar.
int comite 7 regē . Pret hæc habeƀ . xx . liƀ . 7 coīn . x . liƀ
de firma burgi . aut plus aut min ſīc poterat collocare
parte ſuā . Molend . i . redđ regi . xl . ſol . comiti . xx . ſol.

9   In the other two quarters there were and are 140 burgesses (with as many houses), less ½ house, liable for all customary dues and for the King's tax. They had 80 sites, for which they gave and give all customary dues. Of these St. Benedict's of Ramsey had 22 (32?)* burgesses before 1066. Two of them were exempt from all customary dues; 30 paid 10d a year each. All other customary dues were the Abbot's, apart from the King's tax.

10   In these quarters before 1066 Aelfric the Sheriff had a residence, which King William afterwards granted to his wife and children. Eustace now has it, but the deprived (son) claims it, with his mother.

11   In these two quarters 44 residences were and are unoccupied; they gave and give their customary dues.

12   Besides these, also in these two quarters, Burgred and Thorkell had one church before 1066, with 2 hides of land and 22 burgesses, with their houses, who belong to this church, with full jurisdiction. Eustace now has them all; wherefore they claim the King's mercy. Nevertheless these 22 burgesses give the King all customary dues.

13   Bishop Geoffrey (of Coutances) has 1 church and 1 house of the above, which Eustace took away from St. Benedict's, which still claims them.

14   In this Borough Gos and Hunef had 16 houses before 1066, with full jurisdiction and market rights. These Countess Judith now has.

15   The Borough of Huntingdon answered for the King's tax for a   203 b
     fourth part of Hurstingstone Hundred, for 50 hides. But it does not now pay tax in that Hundred, since King William placed a mint tax on the Borough.

16   From the whole of this Borough before 1066 £10 went in land-tribute, from which the Earl had a third part and the King two parts. Of these dues 16s 8d now remain on the 20 residences where the castle is,(shared) between the Earl and the King.

17   In addition the King had £20 from the Borough revenue, and the Earl £10, more or less, according to how he could arrange his part. One mill pays 40s to the King, 20s to the Earl.

Ad hc burgū jaceɴ . II . hidæ 7 XL . ac̄ træ . 7 x . ac̄ p̄ti.

unde partiunt rex . II . part . comes tciā.

Hanc trā coluɴ burgenſes 7 locaɴ p miniſtros regis

7 comitis . Infra p̄dic̄tū censū ſuɴ . III . piſcatores . III . ſoł

reddentes . In hoc burgo fuer̄ . III . monetarij . reddentes

XL . ſolid int̄ regē 7 comitē . ſed m̄ non ſuɴ.

T.R.E. reddeƀ xxx . liƀ . m̄ ſimilit̄.

In HERSTINGEST̄ Hđ ſt̄ dn̄icæ car q̄etæ de geldo regis.

Viłłi 7 ſocħi geldant scđm hidas in breui ſcriptas . Excepta

Broc̄tone ubi geldat aƀƀ cū alijs ᵱ una hida.

HIC ANNOTANT̄ TENENTES TERRAS JN HVNTEDVNSCII

.I. REX WILLELMVS.	.XVI. Suain de Exeſſe.
.II. Eƥſ Lincolienſis.	.XVII. Rogerius de Juri.
.III. Eƥſ Conſtantienſis.	.XVIII. Ernulfus de Heſding.
.IIII. Abbatia de Elẏ.	.XIX. Euſtachius uicecomes.
.V. Abbatia de Cruiland.	.XX. Judita comitiſſa.
.VI. Abbatia de Rameſẏ.	.XXI. Giſlebertus de gand.
.VII. Abbatia de Tornẏ.	.XXII. Albericus de Ver.
.VIII. Abbatia de Burg.	.XXIII. Wiłłs filius Anſculfi.
.IX. Comes Euſtachius.	.XXIIII. Rannulf fr̄ Ilgerij.
.X. Comes de Ow.	.XXV. Roƀtus Faſiton.
.XI. Comes Hugo.	.XXVI. Wiłłs ingania.
.XII. Walterius Gifard.	.XXVII. Radulfus filius oſmund.
.XIII. Wiłłs de Warenna.	.XXVIII. Rohais uxor Ricardi.
.XII. Hugo de Bolebech.	.XXIX. Taini Regis.
.XV. Eudo filius huberti.	

18   In (the lands of) this Borough lie 2 carucates* and 40 acres of land, and 10 acres of meadow; the tribute thereof is shared, the King two parts and the Earl the third part. The burgesses cultivate this land and let it through the officers of the King and the Earl. Among the said dues, 3 fishermen who pay 3s.

19   In this Borough were 3 moneyers who paid 40s, shared between the King and the Earl; but they are not there now.

20   Before 1066 it paid £30; now the same.

21*   In Hurstingstone Hundred the lordship ploughs* are exempt from the King's tax. The villagers and Freemen pay tax according to the hides entered in the records, except in Broughton, where the Abbot* pays tax with the rest for 1 hide.

LIST OF LANDHOLDERS IN HUNTINGDONSHIRE

1	King William	16	Swein of Essex
2	The Bishop of Lincoln	17	Roger of Ivry
3	The Bishop of Coutances	18	Arnulf of Hesdin
4	Ely Abbey	19	Eustace the Sheriff
5	Crowland Abbey	20	Countess Judith
6	Ramsey Abbey	21	Gilbert of Ghent
7	Thorney Abbey	22	Aubrey de Vere
8	Peterborough Abbey	23	William son of Ansculf
9	Count Eustace	24	Ranulf brother of Ilger
10	The Count of Eu	25	Robert Fafiton
11	Earl Hugh	26	William the Artificer
12	Walter Giffard	27	Ralph son of Osmund
13	William Warenne	28	Rohais wife of Richard
14	Hugh of Bolbec	29	The King's Thanes
15	Eudo son of Hubert		

.I. TERRA REGIS.   *HERTINGSTAN HD̄.*

M̃ **I**n *HEREFORDE* habuit rex EDVV . xv . hidas

    tre ad glđ . Tra xvii . car̄ . Rannulf ^{fr Ilgerij} m̃ cuſtodit.

Ibi nc̄ in dn̄io . iiii . car̄ . 7 xxx . uiłł . 7 iii . borđ.

hn̄t . viii . car̄ . Ibi pbr 7 ii . æcclæ . 7 ii . moſini . iiii . lib

7 xl . ac̄ p̃ti . Silua paſt . i . lev łg . 7 dim lev lat̄.

T.R.E. uał . xxiiii . lib̄ . m̃ . xv . lib̄. *NORMANECROS*

M̃ **I**n *BOTVLVESBRIGE* . hb̄ rex Edw.   *HVND̄.*

.v . hidas ad glđ . Tra . viii . car̄ . Ibi nc̄ in dn̄io ht̄ rex

i . car̄ . 7 xv . uiłł hn̄tes . v . car̄ . Ibi pbr 7 æccła . 7 lx

ac̄ p̃ti . 7 xii . ac̄ ſiluæ paſtił in hanteſcy̆re . T.R.E.

uał . c . ſoł . m̃ . viii . lib̄ . Rannulf ⁹ cuſtodit.

In hoc M̄ ^{H regis} | 7 in alijs manerijs . necat excluſa abbatis ^{de Torni}

ccc . acras p̃ti.

In Stichiltone hn̄t ſochi regis ^{de Normanecros} . iii . uirgatas tre

ad glđ . Tra . ii . car̄ . 7 v . bou arantes.

In Ouretune ht̄ rex ſoc̄a ſup . iii . hid trǣ 7 dimiđ.

jn tra abb̄is de Burg . quæ fuit Goduini.

M̃ **I**n *GRANTESDENE* . hb̄ Algarus . ^{com̄} *TOLESLVND HVND̄.*

viii . hidas tre ad glđ . Tra . xv . car̄ . Ibi nc̄ in dn̄io.

vii . car̄ . 7 xxiiii . uiłł 7 viii . borđ hn̄tes . viii . car̄.

Ibi pbr 7 æccła 7 l . ac̄ p̃ti . 7 ſiluæ min̄ xii . ac̄ . De pa

ſtura . v . ſoł 7 iiii . den exeuɴ . T.R.E. uał . xl . lib̄ . m̃ xxx . lib̄.

Rannulf ⁹ cuſtod .   *DE LESTVNE HVND̄.*

M̃ **I**n *ACVMESBERIE* 7 Ged^{Berew}dinge . fuer̄ x . hidæ ad glđ.

Tra . xx . car̄ . Ibi nc̄ ad aul̄a . v . car̄ . in duab hidis

HURSTINGSTONE Hundred

1 M. In HARTFORD King Edward had 15 hides of land taxable.
Land for 17 ploughs. Ranulf brother of Ilger now has
charge of it. Now in lordship 4 ploughs.
    30 villagers and 3 smallholders have 8 ploughs.
      A priest and 2 churches.
      2 mills, £4; meadow, 40 acres; woodland pasture 1 league
        long and ½ league wide.
Value before 1066 £24; now £15.

NORMANCROSS Hundred

2 M. In BOTOLPH BRIDGE King Edward had 5 hides taxable. Land
for 8 ploughs. Now in lordship the King has 1 plough;*
    15 villagers who have 5 ploughs. A priest and a church.
    Meadow, 60 acres; woodland pasture, 12 acres,
      in Northamptonshire.
Value before 1066, 100s; now £8.
    Ranulf has charge of it.
In this manor of the King's and in other manors, a dam
of the Abbot of Thorney drowns 300 acres of meadow.

3 In STILTON the King's Freemen of Normancross have 3 virgates
of land taxable. Land for 2 ploughs; 5 ploughing oxen.*

4 In ORTON* the King has the jurisdiction over 3½ hides of land in
the Abbot of Peterborough's land. It was Godwin's.

TOSELAND Hundred

5 M. In GRANSDEN Earl Algar had 8 hides of land taxable. Land
for 15 ploughs. Now in lordship 7 ploughs;
    24 villagers and 8 smallholders who have 8 ploughs.
      A priest and a church.
    Meadow, 50 acres; underwood, 12 acres; from pasture
      comes 5s 4d.
Value before 1066 £40; now £30.
    Ranulf has charge of it.

LEIGHTONSTONE Hundred*

6 M. In ALCONBURY and its outlier of GIDDING were 10 hides
taxable. Land for 20 ploughs. Now at the hall, 5 ploughs
on 2 hides of this land.

huj træ.7 xxxv . uilli.hnt ibi . xiii . car.7 qt xx.
acs pti . T.R.E. ual . xii . lib . m similit . Rann cuſtodit.

ⵛ In CHETELESTAN hb rex Edw . iiii . hidas træ ad glđ.
Tra . xii . car. Ibi nc in dnio . ii . car.7 xxiiii . uill 7 viii.
borđ hnt x . car 7 qt xx.7 vi . ac pti . Silue paſt p loca
v . q̷ lg 7 i . q̷ 7 dim lat. T.R.E.7 m ual x . lib . Rann cuſtod.

ⵛ In BRANTVNE . hb rex Edw. xv . hid ad glđ. Tra
xv.car. Ibi m . iii . car.7 xxxvi . uill.7 ii . borđ . hnt
xii . car. Ibi æccla 7 pbr.7 c . ac pti. Silua paſt dim
lev lg.7 ii . q̷ lat.7 ii . molini redđ . c . ſolid. T.R.E.7 m
ual . xx . lib . Rann cuſtod.   ꟼ in Leſtuneſtan hđ.

S In Grafhā . ſunt . v . hidæ ad glđ. Tra . viii . car. Soca
Ibi m vii . ſochi 7 xvii . uilli hnt . vi . car.7 vi . acs pti.
Silua paſt . i . lev lg.7 i . lat. T.R.E. ual . v . lib . m . x . ſol min.

ⵛ In GODMVNDCESTRE . hb rex Edw . xiiii . hid ad glđ.
Tra . lvii . car. Ibi m . ii . car in dnio regis . in . ii . hid huj træ.
7 qt xx uilli hnt . xxiiii . car. Ibi pbr 7 æccla.7 iii . molini
c . ſolid 7 clx . ac pti.7 l ac ſiluæ paſt. De paſtura . xx . ſol.
De ptis . lxx . ſol. T.R.E. ual xl . lib . m ſimil ad numerū.

203 d .II. TERRA EPI LINCOLIENS. TOLESLVND HVND.
ⵛ In COTES hb eps de Lincolia . ii . hiđ ad glđ. Tra
iii . car. Ibi m in dnio . ii . car.7 iii . uill hntes   boues
7 xx . ac pti. T.R.E.7 m ual xl . ſol. Turſtin tenet de epo.

35 villagers have 13 ploughs.
Meadow, 80 acres.
Value before 1066 £12; now the same.
Ranulf brother of Ilger has charge of it.

7 M. In KEYSTON King Edward had 4 hides of land taxable. Land for 12 ploughs. Now in lordship 2 ploughs.
24 villagers and 8 smallholders have 10 ploughs.
Meadow, 86 acres; woodland pasture in various places, 5 furlongs long and 1½ furlongs wide.
Value before 1066 and now £10.
Ranulf brother of Ilger has charge of it.

8 M. In BRAMPTON King Edward had 15 hides taxable. Land for 15 ploughs. Now 3 ploughs there.
36 villagers and 2 smallholders have 14 ploughs. A church and a priest.
Meadow, 100 acres; woodland pasture ½ league long and 2 furlongs wide; 2 mills which pay 100s.
Value before 1066 and now £20.
Ranulf brother of Ilger has charge of it.

9 S. In GRAFHAM are 5 hides taxable. Land for 8 ploughs.
Jurisdiction in Leightonstone Hundred.
Now 7 Freemen and 17 villagers have 6 ploughs.
Meadow, 6 acres; woodland pasture 1 league long and 1 wide.
Value before 1066 £40; now the same, (in coin) at face value.

10 M. In GODMANCHESTER King Edward had 14 hides taxable. Land for 57 ploughs. Now 2 ploughs in the King's lordship, on 2 hides of land.
80 villagers and 16 smallholders have 24 ploughs. A priest and a church.
3 mills, 100s; meadow, 160 acres; woodland pasture 50 acres; from pasture 20s; from meadows 70s.
Value before 1066 £40; now the same, (in coin) at face value.

2   LAND OF THE BISHOP OF LINCOLN   203 d

TOSELAND Hundred
1 M. In COTTON the Bishop of Lincoln had 2 hides taxable. Land for 3 ploughs. Now in lordship 2 ploughs;
3 villagers who have 2* oxen.
Meadow, 20 acres.
Value before 1066 and now 40s.
Thursten holds from the Bishop.

꜔ In *TOCHESTONE* ħƀ eps Lincolie vi . hiđ ad glđ.

Tra . xv . cař . Ibi nc̄ in dn̄io . ii . cař 7 dim . 7 xvi.

uiłłi 7 v̄ . borđ hn̄tes . viii . cař . Ibi pƀr 7 eccła.

7 xxiiii . ac̄ p̃ti . 7 c . ac̄ siluæ past̄ . T.R.E . 7 m̄ uał x . liƀ

Euftaci tenet de epo . Aƀƀ de Ramefy clam fup epm̄ ħ ꜔

꜔ In *DODINTONE* ħƀ eps Lincoliæ . ii . hiđ 7 dim ad glđ.

Tra . ii . cař . Ibi nc̄ in dn̄io . ii . cař . 7 v . uiłł hn̄tes . ii . cař.

Ibi æccła . 7 . xviii . ac̄ prati . Silua past̄ʒdimiđʒlev lḡ . 7 dim lat̄ . T.R.E . uał . lx . fol

Wiłłs tenet de epo .   ⌐m̄ . lxx . fol

꜔ In *BVGEDENE* . ħƀ eps Lincoliæ . xx . hiđ ad glđ.

Tra . xx . cař . Ibi nc̄ in dn̄io . v . cař 7 xxx.vii . uiłł

7 xx . borđ hn̄tes xiiii . cař . Ibi æccła 7 pƀr . 7 i . molin

xxx . foliđ . 7 q̃t xx 7 iiii . ac̄ p̃ti . Silua past̄ . i . lev lḡ.

7 i . lev lat̄ . T.R.E . uał . xx . liƀ . m̄ xvi . liƀ . 7 x . foliđ.

NORMANECROS HVND.

꜔ In *DENTONE* . ħƀ Godricus . v . hiđ ad glđ . Tra . ii . cař.

Ibi m̄ . i . cař in dn̄io 7 x . uiłł 7 ii . borđ hn̄t . v . cař

Ibi æccła 7 pƀr . 7 xx.iiii . ac̄ p̃ti . 7 xxiiii . ac̄ siluæ min.

T.R.E . uał . c . fol . m̄ . iiii . liƀ . Turftin tenet de epo.

꜔ In *OVRETONE* . ħƀ Leuric . iii . hiđ 7 i . uirg træ ad glđ.

Tra . ii . cař 7 i . bcu . Ibi nc̄ in dn̄io . i . cař . 7 ii . uiłłi . 7 ix.

ac̄ p̃ti . T.R.E . uał . xx . fol . m̄ . x . fol . Jołs tenet de epo.

De hac tra clamat rex foca.

꜔ In *STICILTONE* ħƀ Toui . ii . hiđ ad glđ . Tra . ii . cař.

7 vii . bou . Ibi nc̄ in dn̄io . i . cař . 7 vi . uiłł cu̅ . iii . cař.

7 xvi . ac̄ p̃ti . 7 v . ac̄ siluæ min . T.R.E . 7 m̄ uał xl . fol.

K

2 M. In STAUGHTON the Bishop of Lincoln had 6 hides taxable.
Land for 15 ploughs. Now in lordship 2½ ploughs;
16 villagers and 4* smallholders who have 8 ploughs.
A priest and a church.
Meadow, 24 acres; woodland pasture, 100 acres.
Value before 1066 and now £10.
Eustace holds from the Bishop.
The Abbot of Ramsey claims this manor from the Bishop.

3 M. In DIDDINGTON the Bishop of Lincoln had 2½ hides taxable.
Land for 2 ploughs. Now in lordship 2 ploughs;
5 villagers who have 2 ploughs. A church.
Meadow, 18 acres; woodland pasture ½ league long and ½ wide.
Value before 1066, 60s; now 70s.
William holds from the Bishop.

4 M. In BUCKDEN the Bishop of Lincoln had 20 hides taxable.
Land for 20 ploughs. Now in lordship 5 ploughs;
37 villagers and 20 smallholders who have 14 ploughs.
A church and a priest.
1 mill, 30s; meadow, 84 acres; woodland pasture 1 league
long and 1 league wide.
Value before 1066 £20; now £16 10s.

NORMANCROSS Hundred
5 M. In DENTON Godric had 5 hides taxable. Land for 2 ploughs.
Now 1 plough in lordship;
10 villagers and 2 smallholders have 5 ploughs. A church
and a priest.
Meadow, 24 acres; underwood 24 acres.
Value before 1066, 100s; now £4.
Thursten holds from the Bishop.

6 M. In ORTON* Leofric had 3 hides and 1 virgate of land taxable.
Land for 2 ploughs and 1 ox. Now in lordship 1 plough;
2 villagers.
Meadow, 9 acres.
Value before 1066, 20s; now 10s.
K   John holds from the Bishop. The King claims the
jurisdiction of this land.

7 M. In STILTON Tovi had 2 hides taxable. Land for 2 ploughs
and 7 oxen. Now in lordship 1 plough;
6 villagers with 3 ploughs.
Meadow, 16 acres; underwood, 5 acres.
Value before 1066 and now 40s.

Joħs tenet de epo.Ħ ꞇra fuit data Vluuino epo .T.R.E.

ᴔ In *LECTONE* ħɓ Turchill.xv . hiđ ad glđ . Tra
xvii . car . Ibi nc in dnio . vi . car . 7 xxx.iii . uiłħ 7 iii . borđ
hntes . x . car . 7 i . moliħ . iii . foliđ . De hac ꞇra tenen̛
iii . milites . iii . hiđ . i . uirg min . Ibi hnt . iii . car . 7 iii . uiłħ
cū dim car . Ibi . xxx . ac p̃ti . 7 x . ac filuæ min . T.R.E.
7 m̊ dniū epi uał . xx . liɓ . Tra militū . Lx . fol .
Hoc ᴔ dcđ Wałłef in elemofiħ S̃ MARIÆ de Lincoł .
In Partenhale . ħɓ Aluuin . i . uirg ꞇræ ad glđ . Tra
dim car . Ħ ꞇra fita . e in Bedefordefcire . fed glđ 7 fer
uitiū reddit in hontedunefcyre . Hanc clamant mi
niftri regis ad op̃ ipfius . T.R.E. 7 m̊ uał . v . fol . Wiłłs
tenet de epo . R . 7 arat ibi cū fuo dnio

K

.III. TERRA EP̃I CONSTANTIENS̃.
In *EREGRAVE* ħɓ Semar . i . uirg ꞇre ad glđ . Tra
ii boū . Soca in Lectuneftan . Idem ipfe nc tenet
de epo conftantienfi . 7 arat ibi cū . ii . boɓ . 7 hŧ . ii . acs
p̃ti . T.R.E. uał v . fol . m̊ fimiliŧ .

.IIII. TERRA ABBATIÆ DE ELÿG. *HERSTINGST̛*
ᴔ In *COLNE* ħɓ aɓɓ de Elÿ . vi . hiđ ad glđ . Tra . vi . car . *HVNĐ.*
7 in dnio ꞇra . ii . caruc̛ . Ibi m̊ in dnio . ii . car . 7 xiii .
Exceptis . vi . hiđ.
uiłł . 7 v . borđ hntes . v . car . 7 x . ac p̃ti . Silua paft
.i . lev łg . 7 dim laŧ . 7 marefc tantunđ . T.R.E. uał . vi . liɓ.
m̊ . c . foliđ .

John holds from the Bishop. This land was given to Bishop Wulfwy* before 1066.

LEIGHTONSTONE Hundred

8 M. In LEIGHTON Thorkell the Dane had 15 hides taxable. Land for 17 ploughs. Now in lordship 6 ploughs;
> 33 villagers and 3 smallholders who have 10 ploughs. 1 mill, 3s.
>> 3 men-at-arms hold 3 hides of this land, less 1 virgate. They have 3 ploughs and 3 villagers with ½ plough.
> Meadow, 30 acres; underwood, 10 acres.

Value of the Bishop's lordship before 1066 and now £20; of the men-at-arms' land 60s.
> Earl Waltheof gave this manor in alms to St. Mary's of Lincoln.

9 In PERTENHALL Alwin had 1 virgate of land taxable. Land for ½ plough.

K
> This land is situated in Bedfordshire, but it pays tax and service in Huntingdonshire. The King's officers claim it for his work.

Value before 1066 and now 5s.
> William holds it from Bishop Remigius and ploughs there, together with his lordship.

3   LAND OF THE BISHOP OF COUTANCES   204 a

[LEIGHTONSTONE Hundred]

1 M. In HARGRAVE Saemer had 1 virgate of land taxable. Land for 2 oxen. Jurisdiction in Leightonstone. Now he still holds it himself from the Bishop of Coutances. He ploughs there with 2 oxen and has 2 acres of meadow.
Value before 1066, 5s; now the same.

4   LAND OF ELY ABBEY*

HURSTINGSTONE Hundred

1 M. In COLNE the Abbot* of Ely had 6 hides taxable. Land for 6 ploughs. Apart from the 6 hides, land* in lordship for 2 ploughs. Now in lordship 2 ploughs;
> 13 villagers and 5 smallholders who have 5 ploughs.
> Meadow, 10 acres; woodland pasture 1 league long and ½ wide; marsh, as much.

Value before 1066 £6; now 100s.

ꝳ In *Blvntesha̅*. ħɓ abɓ de Elẏ. vi. hiđ 7 dim̅ ad glđ.
Tra. viii. car̅. 7 exceptis his hidis: in dn̅io tra̅. ii. car.
Ibi n̅c in dn̅io. ii. car. 7 x. uiłł 7 iii. borđ cū. iii. car̅.
Ibi pɓr 7 æccła. 7 xx. ac̅ p̅ti. Silua paſt. i. leu̅ łg̅.
7 iiii. q̃ᷓ lat̅. T.R.E. 7 m̅ uał. c. ſolid̅.

ꝳ In *Svmersham*. ħɓ abɓ de Elẏ. viii. hiđ ad glđ.
Tra. xii. car̅. 7 exceptis his hiđ in dn̅io tra̅. ii. car̅.
Ibi n̅c in dn̅io. ii. car. 7 xxxii. uiłł 7 ix. borđ hn̅tes
ix. car̅. Ibi. iii. piſcinæ. viii. ſolid̅. 7 xx. ac̅ p̅ti. Silua
paſt. i. leu̅ łg̅. 7 vii. q̃ᷓ lat̅. T.R.E. uał. vii. liɓ. m̅ viii. liɓ.

ꝳ In *Spaldvice*. ħɓ abɓ de Elẏ. xv. hiđ ad glđ.
Tra. xv. car̅. Ibi n̅c in dn̅io. iiii. car̅ in. v. hiđ iſti
træ. 7 l. uiłł. 7 x. borđ hn̅tes. xxv. car̅. Ibi. i.
molin̅. ii. ſolidoᷓ. 7 clx. ac̅ p̅ti. 7 lx. ac̅ filuæ paſt.
T.R.E. uał. xvi. liɓ. m̅. xxii. liɓ.

ꝳ In parua Cateuuorde *Beʀ*. de Spalduice. iiii. hiđ
ad glđ. Tra. iiii. car̅. Ibi m̅. vii. uiłłi. hn̅t. ii. car̅.

.V. Terra Abbatie De Crviland.

ꝳ In *Morbvrne* ħɓ abɓ de Cruilande. v. hiđ ad glđ.
Tra. ix. car̅. Ibi n̅c in dn̅io. ii. car̅. in una hida huj træ.
7 xvi. uiłł 7 iii. borđ hn̅tes. vii. car̅. Ibi æccła 7 pɓr.
7 xl. ac̅ p̅ti. 7 i. ac̅ filuæ min̅. T.R.E. 7 m̅ uał. c. ſolid̅.
In Torninge. i. hiđ 7 dim ad glđ. Tra. i. car̅ 7 dimid.
Soca in Acumeſberie ꝳ regis. Euſtachius m̅ tenet
de abɓe de Cruiland 7 ħt ibi. i. car̅. 7 i. uiłł cū dim car̅.
7 vi. ac̅s p̅ti. T.R.E. 7 m̅ uał. xx. ſoł.

204 a

2 M. In **BLUNTISHAM** the Abbot of Ely had 6½ hides taxable. Land
 for 8 ploughs. Apart from these hides, land in lordship
 for 2 ploughs. Now in lordship 2 ploughs;
   10 villagers and 3 smallholders with 3 ploughs. A priest
    and a church.
   Meadow, 20 acres; woodland pasture 1 league long and
    4 furlongs wide.
 Value before 1066 and now 100s.

3 M. In **SOMERSHAM** the Abbot of Ely had 8 hides taxable. Land
 for 12 ploughs. Apart from these hides, land in lordship
 for 2 ploughs. Now in lordship 2 ploughs;
   32 villagers and 9 smallholders who have 9 ploughs.
   3 fishponds, 8s; meadow, 20 acres; woodland pasture 1
    league long and 7 furlongs wide.
 Value before 1066 £7; now £8.

[LEIGHTONSTONE Hundred]
4 M. In **SPALDWICK** the Abbot of Ely had 15 hides taxable. Land
 for 15 ploughs. Now in lordship 4 ploughs on 5 hides of this land;
   50 villagers and 10 smallholders who have 25 ploughs.
   1 mill, 2s; meadow, 160 acres; woodland pasture, 60 acres.
 Value before 1066 £16; now £22.

5 M. In **LITTLE CATWORTH**, an outlier of Spaldwick, 4 hides taxable.
   Land for 4 ploughs.
   Now 7 villagers have 2 ploughs.

5   **LAND OF CROWLAND ABBEY**

[NORMANCROSS Hundred]
1 M. In **MORBORNE** the Abbot of Crowland had 5 hides taxable.
   Land for 9 ploughs. Now in lordship 2 ploughs on 1 hide
   of this land;
   16 villagers and 3 smallholders who have 7 ploughs. A
    church and a priest.
   Meadow, 40 acres; underwood, 1 acre.
 Value before 1066 and now 100s.

[LEIGHTONSTONE Hundred]
2   In **THURNING** 1½ hides of land taxable. Land for 1½ ploughs.
   Jurisdiction in the King's manor of Alconbury. Eustace
   now holds from the Abbot of Crowland. He has 1 plough;
   1 villager with ½ plough.
   Meadow, 6 acres.
 Value before 1066 and now 20s.

204 b **.VI.** ȝ TERRA SCĪ BENEDICTI. *HERSTINGESTAN HVND.*

In STIVECLE . h̄ḃ aḃḃ de Ramefý . vii . hiḋ ad glḋ.

T̄ra xi . car̄ . Exceptis his hiḋ in dn̄io t̄ra . ii . car̄.

Ibi nc̄ in dn̄io . ii . car̄ . 7 xvi . uiłłis 7 ii . borḋ hn̄tes . vi . car̄.

Ibi æccła 7 pḃr . 7 xxiiii . ac̄ p̄ti . Silua paſt . iiii.

q̇ʒ lḡ . 7 iii . laṫ . T.R.E. uał . vi . liḃ . m̄ . iiii . liḃ 7 x . ſoł.

De hac t̄ra hn̄t . ii . milites aḃḃis Ricarḋ 7 Hugo

iii . hiḋ . 7 ibi hn̄t . iii . car̄ in dn̄io . 7 uał . xxx . ſolid.

In RIPTVNE . h̄ḃ aḃḃ de Ramefý . x . hiḋ ad glḋ.

T̄ra . xvi . car̄ . 7 in dn̄io t̄ra . ii . car̄ . ext̄ p̄dictas hiḋ.

Ibi nc̄ in dn̄io . ii . car̄ . 7 xxvii . uiłł 7 vi . borḋ hn̄tes

x̄ii . car̄ . Ibi æccła 7 pḃr . 7 xvi . ac̄ p̄ti . Silua paſt

. i . leṽ lḡ . 7 i . leṽ laṫ . T.R.E. 7 m̄ uał . viii . liḃ.

In BROGTVNE . h̄ḃ aḃḃ de Ramefý . iiii . hiḋ ad glḋ.

T̄ra . vii . car̄ 7 ii . boū . Ibi t̄ra ſocho̔ʒ . v . hiḋ ad glḋ.

T̄ra . viii . car̄ . 7 vi . boū . Iſti ſochi dicunt ſe habuiſſe

Legreuuitā 7 blodeuuitā . 7 Latrociniū ſq̄ ad . iiii . den.

7 poſt . iiii . denar̄ habeḃ aḃḃ forisfactūra latrocinij.

Nc̄ in dn̄io h̄t aḃḃ . iiii . car̄ . 7 x . ſocłt 7 xx . uiłł hn̄tes

. x . car̄ . Ibi pḃr 7 æccła . 7 i . moliñ . iii . ſolid 7 x . ac̄ p̄ti.

Silua paſt . iii . q̇ʒ lḡ . 7 ii . laṫ . T.R.E. uał . ix . liḃ . m̄ . x . liḃ.

Euſtachi calūniaṫ . v . hiḋ

In WISTOV . h̄ḃ aḃḃ de Ramefý . ix . hiḋ ad gld . T̄ra

xvi . car̄ . 7 t̄ra . iii . car̄ in dn̄io p̄ter ipſas hiḋ . Ibi nc̄

in dn̄io . ii . car̄ . 7 xxxii . uiłł . hn̄tes . xi . car̄ . Ibi pḃr 7 æccła.

7 i . moliñ . ii . ſolido̔ʒ . 7 xxiiii . ac̄ p̄ti . Silua paſt . i . leṽ

lḡ . 7 dim laṫ . T.R.E. uał ix . liḃ . m̄ . viii . liḃ.

In VPEHVDE . h̄ḃ aḃḃ de Ramefý . x . hiḋ ad gld.

T̄ra . xvi . car̄ . 7 in dn̄io t̄ra . iii . car̄ . p̄ter p̄dictas hiḋ.

K

The Abbot of Ramsey had*
HURSTINGSTONE Hundred

1 M. in STUKELEY 7 hides taxable. Land for 11 ploughs. Apart from these hides, land* in lordship for 2 ploughs. Now in lordship 2 ploughs;
>   16 villagers and 2 smallholders who have 6 ploughs.
>   A church and a priest.
>   Meadow, 24 acres; woodland pasture 4 furlongs long
>   and 3 wide.
> Value before 1066 £6; now £4 10s.
>   Two of the Abbot's men-at-arms, Richard and Hugh, have 3 hides of this land. They have 3 ploughs in lordship. Value 30s.

2 M. in (ABBOTS) RIPTON 10 hides taxable. Land for 16 ploughs. As well as the said hides, land in lordship for 2 ploughs. Now in lordship 2 ploughs;
>   27 villagers and 6 smallholders who have 12 ploughs.
>   A church and a priest.
>   Meadow, 16 acres; woodland pasture 1 league long
>   and 1 league wide.
> Value before 1066 and now £8.

3 M. in BROUGHTON 4 hides taxable. Land for 7 ploughs and 2 oxen.
>   Freemen's land, 5 hides taxable. Land for 8 ploughs and 6 oxen.
>   These Freemen state that they had the fines from adultery
>   and bloodshed, and from their* robbery up to 4d; over 4d the
>   Abbot had the fines from robbery.
> Now the Abbot has 4 ploughs in lordship;
>   10 Freemen and 20 villagers who have 10 ploughs.
>   A priest and a church.
>   1 mill, 3s; meadow, 10 acres; woodland pasture 3 furlongs
>   long and 2 wide.
> Value before 1066 £9; now £10.
>   Eustace claims 5 hides. *

K

4 M. in WISTOW 9 hides taxable. Land for 16 ploughs. Besides these hides, land for 3 ploughs in lordship. Now in lordship 2 ploughs;
>   32 villagers who have 11 ploughs. A priest and a church.
>   1 mill, 2s; meadow, 24 acres; woodland pasture 1 league
>   long and ½ wide.
> Value before 1066 £9; now £8.

5 M. in UPWOOD 10 hides taxable. Land for 16 ploughs.

Ibi nc̄ in dn̄io . II . car̄ .7 XXXII . uill 7 II . borđ cū . XIIII . car̄.

Ibi p̄br 7 æccła .7 VI . ac̄ p̄ti . Silua past̄ . I . leu̅ 7 dim lḡ.

7 I . lat̄ . T.R.E. ual̄ . X . liƀ . m̄ . IX . liƀ.

⊗ In *HALIEWELLE* . h̄ƀ abƀ de Ramesẏ . IX . hiđ ad glđ.

Tra . IX . car̄ .7 in dn̄io trā . II . car̄ . p̄ter p̄dictas hiđ.

Ibi nc̄ in dn̄io . II . car̄ .7 XXVI . uill 7 III . borđ cū . VI . car̄.

Ibi æccła 7 p̄br .7 XXX . ac̄ p̄ti . Silua past̄ . I . leu̅ lḡ .7 II . q̄z̧.

7 I . leu̅ lat̄ . Maresc . I . leu̅ lḡ .7 I . lat̄ . T.R.E. 7 m̄ ual̄ . VIII . liƀ.

De hac tra h̄t Aluuold de abƀe . I . hiđ .7 ibi h̄t . I . car̄.

7 III . borđ . Valet . X . soliđ.

⊗ In *SLEPE* . h̄ƀ abƀ de Ramesẏ . XX . hiđ ad glđ . Tra

XXIIII . car̄ .7 in dn̄io trā . III . car̄ . ext p̄dictas hidas.

Ibi nc̄ in dn̄io . III . car̄ .7 XXXIX . uilłi 7 XII . borđ h̄ntes

XX . car̄ . Ibi p̄br 7 æccła .7 LX . ac̄ p̄ti . Silua pastił

. I . leu̅ lḡ .7 dim lat̄ . T.R.E. ual̄ . XX . liƀ . m̄ . XVI . liƀ.

204 c

De hac tra hn̄t . III . hōes abƀis Eurard Ingelrann

7 Pleines . IIII . hiđ .7 ipsi h̄nt ibi . III . car̄ 7 dim.

7 V . uilłi 7 VI . borđ . cū . III . car̄ . Æcclam 7 p̄brm

Valet . XL.V . sol̄ . Eustachi̧ calūn . II . hiđ 7 dim.

⊗ In *HOCTVNE* . h̄ƀ abƀ de Ramesẏ . VII . hiđ ad glđ

Tra . X . car̄ .7 in dn̄io trā . II . car̄ ext p̄dict hiđ.

Ibi nc̄ in dn̄io . II . car̄ .7 XXXI . uill 7 V . borđ cū . X.

car̄ . Ibi æccła n̄ p̄br .7 I . molin . XX . soliđ .7 LX . ac̄

p̄ti . Silua past̄ . I . leu̅ lḡ .7 dim leu̅ lat̄ . T.R.E.

K   7 m̄ ual̄ . VIII . liƀ . Eustachi̧ calūniat . I . hidā.

⊗ In *WITVNE* . h̄ƀ abƀ de Ramesẏ . VII . hiđ ad glđ.

Tra . X . car̄ .7 in dn̄io trā . II . car̄ . ext p̄dict hiđ

Ibi nc̄ in dn̄io . II . car̄ .7 XXIIII . uill 7 V . borđ

h̄ntes . VIII . car̄ . Ibi p̄br 7 æccła .7 I . molin . XII.

soliđ .7 XL . ac̄ p̄ti . T.R.E. 7 m̄ ual̄ . VII . liƀ.

Besides the said hides, land in lordship for 3 ploughs. Now in lordship 2 ploughs;
 32 villagers and 2 smallholders with 14 ploughs.
  A priest and a church.
 Meadow, 6 acres; woodland pasture 1½ leagues long and 1 wide.
Value before 1066 £10; now £9.

6 M. in HOLYWELL 9 hides taxable. Land for 9 ploughs. Besides the said hides, land in lordship for 2 ploughs. Now in lordship 2 ploughs;
 26 villagers and 3 smallholders with 6 ploughs.
  A church and a priest.
 Meadow, 30 acres; woodland pasture 1 league and 4 furlongs
  long and 1 league wide; marsh 1 league long and 1 wide.
Value before 1066 and now £8.
 Alfwold has 1 hide of this land from the Abbot. He has 1 plough and 3 smallholders. Value 10s.

7 M. in ST. IVES* 20 hides taxable. Land for 24 ploughs. As well as the said hides, land in lordship for 3 ploughs. Now in lordship 3 ploughs;
 39 villagers and 12 smallholders who have 20 ploughs.
  A priest and a church.
 Meadow, 60 acres; woodland pasture 1 league long and ½ wide.
Value before 1066 £20; now £16.
 Three of the Abbot's men, Everard, Ingelrann and Pleines,   204 c
have 4 hides of this land. They have 3½ ploughs.
 5 villagers and 6 smallholders with 3 ploughs.
  (They have) the church and the priest.*
K*   Value 45s. Eustace claims 2½ hides.

8 M. in HOUGHTON 7 hides taxable. Land for 10 ploughs. As well as the said hides, land in lordship for 2 ploughs. Now in lordship 2 ploughs;
 31 villagers and 5 smallholders with 10 ploughs. A church, no priest.
 1 mill, 20s; meadow, 60 acres; woodland pasture 1 league
  long and ½ league wide.
Value before 1066 and now £8.
K   Eustace claims 1 hide.

9 M. in WYTON 7 hides taxable. Land for 10 ploughs. As well as the said hides, land in lordship for 2 ploughs. Now in lordship 2 ploughs;
 24 villagers and 5 smallholders who have 8 ploughs.
  A priest and a church.
 1 mill, 12s; meadow, 40 acres.
Value before 1066 and now £7.

In Bluntefhã eft dimid hida ad glđ.Tra.v.boũ.
ptiñ ad ramefỹ.Ibi.ıı.uilli hñt.ı.caɍ.Valet.v.fol.

☾ In *WARDEBVSC* ħɓ aɓɓ de Ramefỹ.x.hid
ad glđ.Tra.xx.caɍ.7 in dñıo trã.ııı.caɍ ext
p̃diĉtas hid.Ibi nc̃ in dñio.ııı.caɍ.7 xxx.ıııı.uilł
7 xııı.borđ hñtes.xvı.caɍ.Ibi pɓr 7 æccła.7 ııı.
ac̃ p̃ti.Silua paſt.ı.leŭ lg̃.7 ı.leŭ lat.Marefc
.ı.leŭ lg̃.7 dim leŭ lat.T.R.E.7 m̃ uał.xıı.liɓ.

NORMANECROS HVND.

☾ In *SALTREDE*.ħɓ aɓɓ de Ramefỹ.vıı.hid 7 dim
7 dim uirg̃ tre ad glđ.Tra.xıı.caɍ.
Ibi nc̃ in dñio.ıı.caɍ.in.ıĩ[ab].hid huj træ.7 xıı.uilł
7 ııı.borđ hñtes.v.caɍ.Ibi æccła 7 pɓr.7 xıı.ac̃ p̃ti.
Silua paſt.ıı.q̃ӡ lg̃.7 ı.q̃ӡ lat.T.R.E.7 m̃ uał.c.fol.

☾ In *ADELINTVNE* ħɓ aɓɓ de Ramefỹ.x.hidas
ad glđ.Tra.xxıııı.caɍ.7 in dñio trã.ıııı.caɍ
ext p̃diĉtas hid.Ibi nc̃ in dñio.ıııı.caɍ.7 xxvııı.
uilli hñtes.xx.caɍ.Ibi æccła 7 pɓr.7 ıı.molini
xL.folid.7 cLxx.ac̃ p̃ti.T.R.E.uał.xıııı.liɓ.m̃

☾ In *LODINTVNE*.ħɓ aɓɓ de Ramefỹ ⌠ xvı.liɓ.
ıı.hid 7 dimid ad glđ.Tra.ıı.caɍ.Ibi nc̃ in dñio
dim caɍ.Edric tenet de aɓɓe.Ibi.xıı.ac̃ p̃ti.T.R.E.
uał.xL.fol.m̃ xx.fol. TOLESLVND HVND.

☾ In *GHELLINGE*.ħɓ aɓɓ de Ramefỹ.v.hid ad glđ.
Tra.vıı.caɍ.Ibi nc̃ in dñio.ıı.caɍ.7 x.uilł 7 ıı.
borđ hñt.ııı.caɍ.Ibi.v.ac̃ p̃ti.T.R.E.7 m̃ uał
ıııı.liɓ.Suiñ teñ de aɓɓe.

☾ In *EMINGEFORDE* ħɓ aɓɓ de Ramefỹ.xvııı.hid
ad glđ.Tra.xvı.caɍ.Ibi nc̃ in dñio.ıı.caɍ.

10 In BLUNTISHAM is ½ hide taxable. Land for 5 oxen, which belongs to Ramsey.

2 villagers have 1 plough.

Value 5s.

The Abbot of Ramsey had*

11 M. in WARBOYS 10 hides taxable. Land for 20 ploughs. As well as the said hides, land in lordship for 3 ploughs. Now in lordship 3 ploughs;

34 villagers and 13 smallholders who have 16 ploughs. A priest and a church.

Meadow, 3 acres; woodland pasture 1 league long and 1 league wide; marsh 1 league long and ½ league wide.

Value before 1066 and now £12.

NORMANCROSS Hundred

12 M. in SAWTRY 7½ hides and ½ virgate of land taxable. Land for 12 ploughs. Now in lordship 2 ploughs on 2 hides of this land;

12 villagers and 3 smallholders who have 5 ploughs. A church and a priest.

Meadow, 12 acres; woodland pasture 2 furlongs long and 1 furlong wide.

Value before 1066 and now 100s.

13 M. in ELTON 10 hides taxable. Land for 24 ploughs. As well as the said hides, land in lordship for 4 ploughs. Now in lordship 4 ploughs;

28 villagers who have 20 ploughs. A church and a priest.

2 mills, 40s; meadow, 170 acres.

Value before 1066 £14; now £16.

14 M. in LUTTON 2½ hides taxable. Land for 2 ploughs. Now in lordship ½ plough.

Edric holds from the Abbot.

Meadow, 12 acres.

Value before 1066, 40s; now 20s.

TOSELAND Hundred

15 M. in YELLING 5 hides taxable. Land for 7 ploughs. Now in lordship 2 ploughs.

10 villagers and 2 smallholders have 3 ploughs.

Meadow, 5 acres.

Value before 1066 and now £4.

Swein holds from the Abbot.

16 M. in HEMINGFORD (ABBOTS) 18 hides taxable. Land for 16 ploughs. Now in lordship 2 ploughs;

7 xxvi . uiłł 7 v . borđ cū . viii . car . Ibi æccıa 7 ɒɒr
7 i . molīn . x . ſolid 7 . viii . deñ . 7 q͛t xx . a͞c p͛ti . T.R.E.
uał . xi . liɓ . m̄ . x . liɓ.

Ⓜ IBIDĒ . ħɓ Godric . i . hid ad glđ . de aɓɓe tenuit . T͛rā
uni car . Modo h͞t Radulf ſili Oſmundi . ſed hõcs
de hund neſciunt p quē . T.R.E. uał . x . ſoł . m̄ . iii . ſoł.

Ⓢ In alia Emingeforde ſu𝔯 . v . hidæ ad glđ . T͛ra . v .
car . SocA in Emingeforde . Nc h͞t Alberic de uer .
de aɓɓe . 7 q͛đā miles h͞t ſub eo . ii . hid huj t͛re . Ibi
in dn̄io . i . car . 7 viii . uiłłi . cū . iii . car . Ibi . xx . a͞c p͛ti
T.R.E. 7 m̄ uał . lx . ſoł . De his fuit . i . hida inland . 7 ſup hoc ⌐ . ii . car in dn̄io

Ⓜ In VPEFORDE . ħɓ aɓɓ de Rameſẏ . iiii . hid ad glđ .
T͛ra . iiii . car . Ibi nc in dn̄io . ii . car . 7 iiii . uiłł . 7 ii . borđ
cū . i . car . 7 xvi . a͞c p͛ti . 7 xvi . a͞c ſiluæ paſt . T.R.E.
7 m̄ uał . iiii . liɓ.

Ⓜ In DELLINCTVNE . ħɓ aɓɓ de Rameſẏ . vi . hid ad glđ .
T͛ra . xii . car . Ibi nc in dn̄io . ii . car . 7 xvi . uiłł hn̄tes
x . car . Ibi . viii . a͞c p͛ti . Silua paſt . i . leʋ 7 . ii . q͛꜀ l͞g .
7 i . leʋ lat . T.R.E. uał . vi . liɓ . m̄ . iiii . liɓ.

DELESTVNE HVNĐ.

Ⓜ In REDINGES . ħɓ aɓɓ de Rameſẏ . i . hid ad glđ .
T͛ra . i . car . H tra fuit in dn̄io . Nc tenet Iunen de aɓɓe .
7 h͞t ibi . i . car . 7 ii . uiłł 7 i . borđ . cū . i . car . 7 vi . a͞cs
p͛ti . T.R.E. 7 m̄ uał . xxx . ſoł.

Ⓜ In BIERNE . ħɓ aɓɓ de Rameſẏ . iiii . hid ad glđ .
T͛ra . iiii . car . Ibi nc in dn̄io . i . car in una hida huj
t͛ræ . 7 xi . uiłł 7 iiii . borđ cū . vii . car . Ibi . xxx . a͞c p͛ti .
T.R.E. uał . c . ſolid . m̄ . iiii . liɓ . De hac t͛ra tenent
ii . milites . iii . uir͛g tre 7 dim̄ de aɓɓe . 7 ibi hn̄t un͞u
uiłłm 7 iii . borđ cū . ii . car . Valet . xxx . ſoł.

26 villagers and 5 smallholders with 8 ploughs.
A church and a priest. .
1 mill, 10s 8d; meadow, 80 acres.
Value before 1066 £11; now £10.

17   There Godric also had 1 hide taxable. He held from the Abbot.
Land for 1 plough. Now Ralph son of Osmund has it, but the
men of the Hundred do not know through whom.
Value before 1066, 10s; now 3s.

18 S.   In the other HEMINGFORD (GREY) are 5 hides taxable. Land for 5
ploughs. Jurisdiction in Hemingford. Now Aubrey de Vere
has it from the Abbot and a man-at-arms has 2 hides of this
land under him. In lordship 1 plough;
8 villagers with 3 ploughs.
Meadow, 20 acres.
Value before 1066 and now 60s.

The Abbot of Ramsey had*

19 M. in OFFORD   4 hides taxable. *Of these 1 hide was *inland* and in
addition thereto there were 2 ploughs in lordship.*   Land
for 4 ploughs. Now in lordship 2 ploughs;
4 villagers and 2 smallholders with 1 plough.
Meadow, 16 acres; woodland pasture, 16 acres.
Value before 1066 and now £4.

20 M. in DILLINGTON   6 hides taxable. Land for 12 ploughs. Now in
lordship 2 ploughs;
16 villagers who have 10 ploughs.
Meadow, 8 acres; woodland pasture 1 league and 2 furlongs
long and 1 league wide.
Value before 1066 £6; now £4.

LEIGHTONSTONE Hundred

21 M. In GIDDING   1 hide taxable. Land for 1 plough. This land was in
lordship. Now Lunen* holds from the Abbot. He has 1 plough;
2 villagers and 1 smallholder with 1 plough.
Meadow, 6 acres.
Value before 1066 and now 30s.

22 M. in BYTHORN   4 hides taxable. Land for 4 ploughs. Now in
lordship 1 plough on 1 hide of this land;
11 villagers and 4 smallholders with 7 ploughs.
Meadow, 30 acres.
Value before 1066, 100s; now £4.
2 men-at-arms hold 3½ virgates of their own land from the Abbot.
They have 1 villager and 3 smallholders with 2 ploughs. Value 30s.

℟ In *BRENINCTVNE* ħƀ abƀ de Ramefy . iiii . hid ad glđ.
Tra . vii . caɼ. Ibi nc̄ in dn̄io . i . caɼ . in una hida huj
tre . 7 xi . uitti 7 iii . borđ. hn̄t . vi . caɼ. Ibi . xl . ac̄
p̄ti. T.R.E. 7 m̄ uat. iiii . liƀ.

℟ In *WESTVNE* . ħƀ abƀ de Ramefy . x . hid ad glđ.
Tra . xiii . caɼ. Ibi nc̄ in dn̄io . ii . caɼ . in . ii . hidis
huj træ . 7 xx . uitt 7 i . borđ hn̄t . vii . caɼ . Ibi p̄ƀr
7 eccta . 7 lx . ac̄ p̄ti . T.R.E. 7 m̄ uat . x . liƀ.

℟ In *REDINGES* . ħƀ abƀ de Ramefy . vii . hiđ ad glđ.
Tra . viii . caɼ. Ibi nc̄ in dn̄io . i . caɼ in una hida huj træ.
7 xviii . uitti hn̄t . vii . caɼ. Ibi . xx . ac̄ p̄ti . 7 Siluæ
min̄ . ii . q̄q̄. T.R.E. 7 m̄ uat . c . fot.

℟ In *ELINTVNE* . ħƀ abƀ de Ramefy . x . hiđ ad glđ.
Tra . xvi . caɼ. De his . x . hiđ . c̄ una wafta p̄ filua

                        regis.

Nc̄ in dn̄io funt ibi . ii . caɼ . in duabʒ hid huj træ.
7 xx. vi . uitt 7 iiii . borđ hn̄t . xii . caɼ. 7 lx . ac̄ p̄ti.
Ibi æccta 7 p̄ƀr. T.R.E. uat . x . liƀ m̄ . ix . liƀ.
De hac tra tenent . ii . milites . i . hiđ . 7 hn̄t . ii . caɼ.
Valet xx . fot.

VII. TERRA S̄ MARIÆ DE TORNI. *NORMANECROS HV̄Nđ.*

℟ In *LACHESLEI* . ħƀ abƀ de Torny . xv . hiđ ad glđ.
Tra . xx . caɼ. Ibi nc̄ in dn̄io . iii . caɼ. 7 xxxviii . uitti
hn̄tes . xviii . caɼ. Ibi æccta 7 p̄ƀr. 7 xxiiii . ac̄ p̄ti . 7 xx.
ac̄ filuæ min̄. T.R.E. uat . xv . liƀ . m̄ xii . liƀ.

℟ In *STANGRVN* . ħƀ abƀ de Torny . viii . hiđ ad glđ.
Tra . x . caɼ. Ibi nc̄ in dn̄io . ii . caɼ in iii . hiđ huj træ.
7 xvi . uitt 7 vi . borđ   Ibi æccta 7 p̄ƀr. 7 xxiiii.
ac̄ p̄ti . 7 vi . ac̄ filuæ min̄. T.R.E. 7 m̄ uat . viii . liƀ.

℟ In *WODESTVN* . ħƀ abƀ de Torny . v . hiđ ad glđ . Tra
ix . caɼ. Ibi nc̄ in dn̄io . ii . caɼ . in una hiđ 7 dim̄ huj træ.

23 M. in BRINGTON 4 hides taxable. Land for 7 ploughs. Now in
   lordship 1 plough on 1 hide of this land.
       11 villagers and 3 smallholders have 6 ploughs.
           Meadow, 40 acres.
   Value before 1066 and now £4.

24 M. in (OLD) WESTON 10 hides taxable. Land for 13 ploughs. Now in
   lordship 2 ploughs on 2 hides of this land.
       20 villagers and 1 smallholder have 7 ploughs.
           A priest and a church.
       Meadow, 60 acres.
   Value before 1066 and now £10.

25 M. in GIDDING 7 hides taxable. Land for 8 ploughs. Now in lordship
   1 plough on 1 hide of this land.
       18 villagers have 7 ploughs.
       Meadow, 20 acres; underwood, 2 furlongs.
   Value before 1066 and now 100s.

26 M. in ELLINGTON 10 hides taxable. Land for 16 ploughs. Of these
       10 hides one is not cultivated, on account of the King's woodland.
       Now in lordship 2 ploughs on 2 hides of this land.   205 a
       26 villagers and 4 smallholders have 12 ploughs.
       Meadow, 60 acres.
       A church and a priest.
   Value before 1066 £10; now £9.
       2 men-at-arms hold 1 hide of this land; they have 2 ploughs .
   Value 20s.

7   LAND OF ST. MARY'S THORNEY

The Abbot of Thorney had*
NORMANCROSS Hundred
1 M. in YAXLEY 15 hides taxable. Land for 20 ploughs. Now
   in lordship 3 ploughs.
       38 villagers who have 18 ploughs. A church and a priest.
       Meadow, 24 acres; underwood, 20 acres.
   Value before 1066 £15; now £12.

2 M. in STANGROUND 8 hides taxable. Land for 10 ploughs. Now in
   lordship 2 ploughs on 3 hides of this land;
       16 villagers and 6 smallholders. A church and a priest.
       Meadow, 24 acres; underwood, 6 acres.
   Value before 1066 and now £8.
3 M. in WOODSTONE 5 hides taxable. Land for 9 ploughs. Now in
   lordship 2 ploughs on 1½ hides of this land.

7 xvi . uilli cū . iiii . car̄ . Ibi æccła 7 p̄br . 7 xvi . ac̄ p̄ti.

7 iiii . ac̄ siluæ min̄ . T.R.E. ual . c . sol . m̄ . iiii . lib̄.

℗ In ADONE . h̄b abb̄ de Torny . v . hid ad glđ . Tra . xii.
car̄ . Ibi nc̄ in dn̄io . ii . car̄ . in una hid 7 dim̄ huj træ.

7 xviii . uilł cū . vi . car̄ . Ibi æccła 7 p̄br . 7 xxiiii . ac̄ p̄ti.

7 i . ac̄ siluæ min̄ . T.R.E. 7 m̄ ual . c . sol.

℗ In NEWETONE . h̄b abb̄ de Torny . v . hid ad glđ . Tra
viii . car̄ . Ibi nc̄ in dn̄io . ii . car̄ . in una hid huj træ.

7 xvi . uilli 7 v . borđ h̄ntes . v . car̄ . Ibi p̄br 7 æccła

7 ii . molini xxxii . soliđ . 7 lx . ac̄ p̄ti . 7 i . c̄suetuđ

in silua abb̄is de Burg . ii . solidoꝛ . T.R.E. ual . v . lib̄ . m̄

℗ In SIBESTVNE . h̄b abb̄ de Torny . ii . hid   𝌆 vii . lib̄.

7 dim̄ ad glđ . Tra . iiii . car̄ . Ibi nc̄ in dn̄io . i . car̄

in una hida huj træ . 7 iiii . uilli cū . i . car̄ . Ibi p̄br

7 dim̄ æccła . 7 dim̄ molin̄ . x . solidoꝛ . 7 xx . ac̄ p̄ti.

T.R.E. 7 m̄ ual . l . sol.

In Stebintone sunt . v . uirḡ træ ad glđ p̄tin ad Sibeftun.
Tra . i . car̄ . Ibi . ē æccła 7 v . uilli cū una car̄ 7 dimid.

7 v . ac̄ p̄ti.

In Witelesmare h̄b abb̄ de Ramesy . i . nauē . 7 abb̄ de
burg . i . nauē . 7 abb̄ de Torny . ii . naues . De his duab̄
ten una abb̄ de burg . 7 ii . piscarias . 7 ii . piscatores . 7 una
uirḡ træ de abbe de Torny . 7 ꝓ his dat paftionē suffici
entē . cxx . porcis . 7 si paftio deficit : de annona pascit

7 impinguat . lx . porcos . Sed & materiē inuenit ad
una domū . lx . peđū . 7 uirgas ad curiā circa domū.
R̄eficit etiā domū 7 curiā si defeceriꞇ . H̄ conuentio
T.R.E. facta . ē int̄ eos.

In Hontedunescire piscariæ 7 maræ abb̄is de Ramesy . p̄ciant
x . lib̄ Abbis de Torny . lx . sol . Abbis de Burg . iiii . lib̄.

16 villagers with 4 ploughs. A church and a priest.
Meadow, 16 acres; underwood, 4 acres.
Value before 1066, 100s; now £4.

4   M. in HADDON 5 hides taxable. Land for 12 ploughs. Now in
lordship 2 ploughs on 1½ hides of this land;
   18 villagers with 6 ploughs. A church and a priest.
   Meadow, 24 acres; underwood, 1 acre.
Value before 1066 and now 100s.

5   M. in (WATER) NEWTON 5 hides taxable. Land for 8 ploughs. Now
in lordship 2 ploughs on 1 hide of this land;
   16 villagers and 5 smallholders who have 5 ploughs.
      A church and a priest.
   2 mills, 32s; meadow, 60 acres; one customary due in the
      Abbot of Peterborough's woodland, 2s.
Value before 1066 £5; now £7.

6   M. in SIBSON 2½ hides taxable. Land for 4 ploughs. Now in lordship
1 plough on 1 hide of this land;
   4 villagers with 1 plough. A priest and half a church.
   ½ mill, 10s; meadow, 20 acres.
Value before 1066 and now 50s.

7   M. In STIBBINGTON are 5 virgates of land taxable, which belong to Sibson.
Land for 1 plough.
   A church. 5 villagers with 1½ ploughs.
   Meadow, 5 acres.

8   M. In WHITTLESEY MERE* the Abbot of Ramsey had 1 boat; the Abbot of
Peterborough 1 boat; and the Abbot of Thorney 2 boats. Of these
two, the Abbot of Peterborough holds one from the Abbot of
Thorney, and also 2 fisheries and 2 fishermen, and 1 virgate of
land. For these he gives pasture sufficient for 120 pigs, and, if
the pasture is inadequate he feeds and fattens 60 pigs with corn.
He also finds materials for one house of 60 feet, and poles for the
court around the house; he also repairs the house and court if
they fall into disrepair. This agreement was made between them
before 1066.
   *The Abbot of Ramsey's fisheries and meres in Huntingdonshire
are assessed at £10; the Abbot of Thorney's at 60s; the Abbot of
Peterborough's at £4.*

ᴍ TERRA S͞ PETRI DE BVRG *NORMANECROS HVND.*

Ⅰn *FLETVN*. h̅b̅ ab̅b̅ de Burg . v . hid ad gl̅d̅ . T̅ra
viii . car̅ . Ibi n̅c̅ in d̅n̅io . ii . car̅ . In una hida 7 dim
huj̅ træ . Ibi . xiiii . uil̅l̅i 7 iii . bord̅ h̅n̅tes . vi . car̅ .
Ibi æccl̅a 7 xl . ac̅ p̅ti . T.R.E. 7 m̅ ual̅ . c . fol̅

ᴍ Ⅰn *ALWOLTVNE* . h̅b̅ ab̅b̅ de Burg . v . hid ad gl̅d̅ .
T̅ra . ix . car̅ . 7 in d̅n̅io t̅ra . ii . car̅ . p̅t has . v . hid .
Ibi n̅c̅ in d̅n̅io . ii . car̅ . 7 xx . uil̅l̅i h̅n̅tes . vii . car̅ .
Ibi . ii . molini . xl . folid̅ . 7 i . pifcaria q̅ngent anguil̅l̅
. v . folid̅ . 7 x . ac̅ p̅ti . T.R.E. 7 m̅ ual̅ . vii . lib̅ .
Ⅰn Ouretune BER huj̅ ᴍ funt v . hid ad gl̅d̅ . T̅ra
iii . car̅ 7 ii . bou̅ . H̅ e̅ de uictu monachoꝛ . N̅c̅ tenet
Anfgered de ab̅b̅e . 7 ibi h̅t̅ . iii . uil̅l̅ cu̅ . i . car̅ . 7 xv .
ac̅s p̅ti .

ᴍ Ⅰn Eade̅ *OVRETVNE* . h̅b̅ Goduin̅ . iii . hid 7 dim
ad gl̅d̅ . T̅ra . ii . car̅ 7 ii . bou̅ . Rex habuit foca fup
hanc t̅ra . Hæc n̅ p̅tinuit ad abbatia̅ . T.R.E. fed in
dieb̅ . W . regis data . e̅ ad æccl̅am S͞ PETRI . N̅c̅ tenet
Anfgered de ab̅b̅e . 7 h̅t̅ ibi . i . car̅ . 7 iii . uil̅l̅ 7 i . bord̅
cu̅ . i . car̅ . 7 ix . ac̅s p̅ti . T.R.E. ual̅ . xl . fol̅ . m̅ . xx . fol̅ .

IX. TERRA EVSTACHIJ COMITIS.

ᴍ Ⅰn *GLATVNE* . h̅b̅ Vlf . viii . hid ad gl̅d̅ . T̅ra xxiiii .
car̅ . Ibi n̅c̅ in d̅n̅io . ii . car̅ . 7 xxiiii . uil̅l̅ 7 x . bord̅
h̅n̅tes . xiiii . car̅ . Ibi æccl̅a 7 p̅b̅r . 7 lx . ac̅ p̅ti . 7 ii .
ac̅ filuæ paft . 7 xx . ac̅ filuæ min̅ . T.R.E. 7 m̅ ual̅

ᴍ Ⅰn *CESTRETVNE* . h̅b̅ Vlf . iiii . hid   ⎰x . lib̅ .
7 dim ad gl̅d̅ . T̅ra . vii . car̅ . Ibi n̅c̅ in d̅n̅io . i . car̅ .
7 vii . uil̅l̅ 7 i . bord̅ cu̅ . iii . car̅ . Ibi . xx . ac̅ p̅ti .
7 confuetud̅ . ii . folidoꝛ in filua ab̅b̅is de Burg .
T.R.E. ual̅ . iiii . lib̅ . m̅ . xl . folid̅ .

8   LAND OF ST. PETER'S OF PETERBOROUGH   205 b

[NORMANCROSS Hundred]

1   M. In FLETTON the Abbot of Peterborough had 5 hides taxable.
Land for 8 ploughs. Now in lordship 2 ploughs on 1½ hides
of this land.
    14 villagers and 3 smallholders who have 6 ploughs.   A church.
    Meadow, 40 acres.
Value before 1066 and now 100s.

2   M. In ALWALTON   the Abbot of Peterborough had 5 hides taxable.
Land for 9 ploughs. In lordship land for 2 ploughs, besides those
5 hides. Now in lordship 2 ploughs;
    20 villagers who have 7 ploughs.
    2 mills, 40s; 1 fishery, 500 eels; meadow, 10 acres.
Value before 1066 and now £7.

3   In ORTON (WATERVILLE) an outlier of this manor, are 5 hides taxable.
Land for 3 ploughs and 2 oxen. It is for the supplies of the
monks. Now Ansgered* holds from the Abbot. He has
3 villagers with 1 plough. Meadow, 15 acres.

4   M. Also in ORTON (WATERVILLE) Godwin had 3½ hides taxable.
Land for 2 ploughs and 2 oxen. The King had the jurisdiction
over this land. It did not belong to the Abbey before 1066,
but in King William's day it was given to St. Peter's Church.
Now Ansgered* holds from the Abbot. He has 1 plough; 3 villagers
and 1 smallholder with 1 plough. Meadow, 9 acres.
Value before 1066, 40s; now 20s.

9   LAND OF COUNT EUSTACE

[NORMANCROSS Hundred]

1   M. In GLATTON Ulf had 8 hides taxable. Land for 24 ploughs.
    Now in lordship 2 ploughs;
    24 villagers and 10 smallholders who have 14 ploughs.
     A church and a priest.
    Meadow, 60 acres; woodland pasture, 2 acres; underwood 20 acres.
Value before 1066 and now £10.

2   M. In CHESTERTON Ulf had 4½ hides taxable. Land for 7 ploughs.
    Now in lordship 1 plough;
    7 villagers and 1 smallholder with 3 ploughs.
    Meadow, 20 acres; a customary due of 2s in the Abbot of
     Peterborough's woodland.
Value before 1066 £4; now 40s.

ꝏ In *SIBESTVNE* . ħɓ Vlf . ɪɪ . hid 7 dim ad glđ . Tra
. ɪɪɪɪ . car . Ibi nc̄ in dn̄io . ɪ . car . 7 ɪɪɪ . uiłł 7 ɪ . borđ.
cū . ɪɪ . car . Ibi dim æccła . 7 dimiđ molin̄ . x . solidoᵷ.
7 xx . ac̄ p̄ti . T.R.E. 7 m̄ uał . ʟ . soliđ.
In Stebintune . fuɲ . v . uirg træ ad glđ p̄tin ad Sibeſtun.
Tra . ɪ . car . Ibi nc̄ . v . uiłłi hūt . ɪ . car 7 dim̄ . 7 v.
ac̄ p̄ti.
Has tras om̄s tenet Lunen de comite Euſtachio.

205 c

X.
ꝏ **TERRA COMITIS DE OW.**

ꝏ In *BVCHESWORDE* . ħɓ Toſti . x . hidas ad glđ.
Tra . xvɪɪɪ . car . H̄ fúit BEREW in parcheſtune.
Nc̄ tenet comes de Ow . 7 ibi h̄t in dn̄io . ɪɪ . car.
in duaɓ hiđ huj træ . 7 xvɪ . uiłł hn̄tes x . car . 7 un̄
faɓ hn̄s . v . ac̄s huj træ . Ibi p̄br 7 æccła . ad quā p̄tin
dim hida huj tre . cū . ɪɪ . uiłłis 7 ɪ . car . Ibi q̄t xx.
ac̄ p̄ti . 7 xxx . ac̄ filuæ min̄ . T.R.E. 7 m̄ uał . x . liɓ.
De hac tra tenet un̄ miles . ɪɪ . hid 7 dim̄ . 7 ibi h̄t
ɪɪɪɪ . uiłł 7 ɪ . borđ cū . v . car . Valet . ɪɪɪ . liɓ.

TERRA HVGONIS COMITIS.

.XI. ꝏ In *OPETVNE* . ħɓ Edgar ɪɪɪɪ . hid ad glđ cū faca 7 foca.
Tra . vɪ . car . Ibi nc̄ in dn̄io . ɪɪ . car . in un̄a hid huj træ
7 xɪɪɪɪ . uiłł 7 v . borđ hn̄tes . vɪɪɪ . car . Ibi æccła 7 p̄br.
7 ɪ . molin̄ . ɪɪɪ . folidoᵷ . 7 ʟ . ac̄ p̄ti . T.R.E. uał . ɪɪɪɪ . liɓ . m̄ v . liɓ.
Fulcui ten̄ de Hugone comite.

ꝏ In *COPEMANEFORDE* . ħɓ Edgar . ɪɪɪɪ . hid ad glđ cū
faca 7 foca . Tra . v . car . Ibi nc̄ in dn̄io . ɪ . car . in dimiđ
hida huj træ . 7 xɪɪɪɪ . uiłł 7 ɪɪ . borđ hn̄t . ɪɪɪ . car . Ibi
æccła 7 p̄br . T.R.E. 7 m̄ uał . ɪɪɪɪ . liɓ . Hunfrid ten̄ de comite ᴴᵘᵍᵒⁿᵉ˙

205 b, c

3 M. In SIBSON Ulf had 2½ hides taxable. Land for 4 ploughs. Now
in lordship 1 plough;
>3 villagers and 1 smallholder with 2 ploughs. Half a church.
>½ mill, 10s; meadow, 20 acres.
Value before 1066 and now 50s.

4 In STIBBINGTON 5 virgates of land taxable, which belong to Sibson.
Land for 1 plough.
>Now 5 villagers have 1½ ploughs.
>Meadow, 5 acres.
Lunen holds all these lands from Count Eustace.

10   LAND OF THE COUNT OF EU   205 c

[LEIGHTONSTONE Hundred]

1 M. In BUCKWORTH Tosti had 10 hides taxable. Land for 18 ploughs.
This was an outlier in Paxton. Now the Count of Eu holds
it and has 2 ploughs in lordship on 2 hides of this land.
>16 villagers who have 10 ploughs; a smith who has 5 acres
>of this land. A priest and a church, to which belongs
>½ hide of this land, with 2 villagers and 1 plough.
>Meadow, 80 acres; underwood, 30 acres.
Value before 1066 and now £10.
A man-at-arms holds 2½ hides of this land. He has 4
villagers and 1 smallholder with 5 ploughs. Value £3.

11   LAND OF EARL HUGH

[LEIGHTONSTONE Hundred]

1 M. In UPTON Edgar had 4 hides taxable, with full jurisdiction. Land
for 6 ploughs. Now in lordship 2 ploughs on 1 hide of this land;
>14 villagers and 5 smallholders who have 8 ploughs.
>A church and a priest.
>1 mill, 3s; meadow, 50 acres.
Value before 1066 £4; now £5.
Fulk holds from Earl Hugh.

2 M. In COPPINGFORD Edgar had 4 hides taxable, with full jurisdiction.
Land for 5 ploughs. Now in lordship 1 plough on ½ hide of this land.
>14 villagers and 2 smallholders have 3 ploughs.
>A church and a priest.
Value before 1066 and now £4.
Humphrey holds from Earl Hugh.

TERRA WALTERIJ GIFARD

.XII. ꝳ **I**n *FOLCHESWORDE* ħɓ Chetelber . v . hiđ ad glđ . Ťra v . car̃ . Ibi nc̃ in dñio . I . car̃ . 7 xvII . uiłł 7 v . borđ cũ vII . car̃ . Ibi . xx . ac̃ p̃ti . Silua pat̃ . vI . q̃ɀ łg̃ . 7 II . q̃ɀ 7 vI . p̃tic̃ lat̃ . T.R.E. ual̃ . c . fol̃ . m̃ . IIII , lib̃ . Hugo tenet de Walterio gifard.

.XIII. TERRA WILLELMI DE WARENE.

ꝳ **I**n *CHENEBALTONE* ħɓ Harold . x . hiđ ad glđ . Ťra . xx . car̃ . Nc̃ tenet Wiłłs de Warenna . 7 ibi hĩ in dñio . v . car̃ . 7 qt xx 7 IIII . uiłł . 7 xxx . vI . borđ cũ . xxv . car̃ . Ibi pɓr 7 æccła . 7 Lxx . ac̃ p̃ti . 7 filua pat̃ . I . lev łg̃ . 7 I . lev lat̃ . Ibi . I . moliñ . v . fol̃ . T.R.E. ual̃ . vII . lib̃ . m̃ . xvI . lib̃ 7 IIII . fol̃. ⌐ Valet xx . fol̃ . De hac tra hñt . II . milites . I . hiđ . 7 ibi hñt . I . car̃ 7 v . boũ .

ꮪ **I**n Caiffet . Allic . III . uirg̃ træ ad glđ . Ťra . vI . boũ . SocA Ibi . I . foch̃ 7 vII . borđ . 7 IIII . ac̃ p̃ti . 7 L . ac̃ filuæ paſtilis .

ꮪ **I**n Suineshefet . III . hiđ 7 dim̃ ad glđ . Ťra . IIII . car̃ . SocA Ibi nc̃ . I . foch̃s 7 vII . uiłłi 7 v . borđ . 7 xvI . ac̃ p̃ti . Silua pat̃ . I . lev łg̃ . 7 IIII . q̃ɀ lat̃ . Valet xL . fol̃ . Euſtaci teñ de

ꮪ **I**n Cateuuorde . I . hiđ ad glđ . Ťra . I . car̃ . SocA . Euſtaci teñ de Wiłło . 7 ibi hĩ dim̃ car̃ . 7 I . borđ cũ . I . boue . 7 I , ac̃ p̃ti . 7 vI . ac̃s filuæ minutæ . Valet . xx . fol̃ .

ꮪ **I**n alia Cateuuorde . I . hida ad glđ . Ťra . I . car̃ . SocA Modo teñ Tored de Wiłło . 7 hĩ ibi . I . car̃ . 7 I . borđ .

12   LAND OF WALTER GIFFARD

[NORMANCROSS Hundred]
1 M. In FOLKESWORTH Ketelbert had 5 hides taxable. Land for 5
    ploughs. Now in lordship 1 plough;
       17 villagers and 5 smallholders with 7 ploughs.
       Meadow, 20 acres; woodland pasture 6 furlongs long and
         2 furlongs 6 perches wide.
    Value before 1066, 100s; now £4.

13   LAND OF WILLIAM OF WARENNE

[KIMBOLTON Hundred*]
1 M. In KIMBOLTON Earl Harold had 10 hides taxable. Land for 20
    ploughs. Now William of Warenne holds it. He had 5 ploughs
    in lordship on 5 hides;
       84 villagers and 36 smallholders with 25 ploughs.
       A priest and a church.
       Meadow, 70 acres; woodland pasture 1 league long and 1 league
         wide; 1 mill, 5s.
    Value before 1066 £7; now £16 4s.
       2 men-at-arms have 1 hide of this land. They have 1 plough
    and 5 oxen. Value 20s.

2 S. In KEYSOE Aellic, 3 virgates of land taxable. Land for 6 oxen.
    In Jurisdiction.
       1 Freeman and 7 smallholders.
       Meadow, 4 acres; woodland pasture 50 acres.

3 S. In SWINESHEAD 3½ hides taxable. Land for 4 ploughs. In Jurisdiction.
       Now 1 Freeman, 7 villagers and 5 smallholders.
       Meadow, 16 acres; woodland pasture 1 league long and
         4 furlongs wide.
    Value 40s.
    Eustace holds from William.

4 S. In CATWORTH 1 hide taxable. Land for 1 plough. In Jurisdiction.
    Eustace holds from William. He has ½ plough;
       1 smallholder with 1 ox.
    Meadow, 1 acre; underwood, 6 acres.
    Value 20s.

205 d

5 S. In the other (LITTLE) CATWORTH 1 hide taxable. Land for 1 plough.
    In Jurisdiction. Now Thored holds from William. He has 1 plough;
       1 smallholder.

7 xii . aē p̃ti . Valet xxx . ſolid . Oñis ħ Soca p̃tiñ
ad Kenebaltone.

.XIIII.   Terra Hvgonis ^{de Bolebec}   *Normanecros Hvnd.*

M̃ In *Waltvne* ħɓ Saxi . v . hid ad glđ . Tra . vii . car.
Ibi nē in dñio . ii . car . in una hida huj træ . 7 xix . uiłł.
hñtes . iiii . car . Ibi æccła 7 xvi . aē p̃ti . Silua paſtił
xvi . q̃ʒ lḡ . 7 vi . q̃ʒ 7 ii . uirg lat̃ . T.R.E. 7 m̃ uał . c . ſoł,
Hugo de bolebec tenet de comite Wiłło.

.XV.   Terra Evdon Filij Hvberti.

M̃ In *Hambertvne* ħɓ Vlfech . xv . car træ ad glđ.
Nē ħ Eudo dapifer de rege . 7 Alich 7 Leuuine . iii.
hid Soca in Lectuneſtane hund . hanc tra ħ Eudo
7 rex ħ Soca . Nē in manerio ſunt . iiii . car in dñio
in . iii . hid huj træ . 7 xx . vi . uiłłi hñtes . vi . car . Ibi
lx . aē p̃ti . 7 x . aē ſiluæ min . De hac tra teneɴ . ii . mi
lites . ii . hidas . 7 ibi hñt . ii . car . Totū ħ M̃ T.R.E. uał
xii . liɓ . m̃ ſimilit̃.

     Terra Svain De Exesse *Toleslvnt Hvnd.*
.XVI M̃ In *Wedreslei* . ħɓ Roɓt fili Wimarc . vii . hid
ad glđ . Tra . ix . car . Ibi nē in dñio . ii . car . 7 xvii . uiłł
7 iiii . borđ . cū . ii . car . Ibi xxv . aē p̃ti . 7 xvi . aē ſiluæ
minutæ . T.R.E. uał . viii . liɓ . m̃ . vi . liɓ . Turoldus ten
de Suino de Exeſſe.

.XVII.   Terra Rogerij De Jvri *Delestvne Hvnd.*
M̃ In *Covintvne* . ħɓ Aſchil . viii . hid 7 dim ad glđ.
Tra . xiii . car . Ibi nē in dñio . iii . car in dim car huj træ.
7 xviii . uiłł hñtes . viii . car . Ibi xlviii . aē p̃ti.

Meadow, 12 acres.
Value 30s.
All this Jurisdiction belongs to Kimbolton.

14   LAND OF HUGH OF BOLBEC

NORMANCROSS Hundred
1 M. In (WOOD) WALTON Saxi had 5 hides taxable. Land for 7 ploughs.
    Now in lordship 2 ploughs on 1 hide of this land;
       19 villagers who have 4 ploughs. A church.
       Meadow, 16 acres; woodland pasture 16 furlongs long
          and 6 furlongs and 2 virgates wide.*
    Value before 1066 and now 100s.
       Hugh of Bolbec holds from Earl* William.

15   LAND OF EUDO SON OF HUBERT

[LEIGHTONSTONE Hundred]
1 M. In HAMERTON Wulfheah had 15 carucates of land (hides)* taxable.
    Eudo the Steward now has them from the King. *Aellic and
    Leofwin 3 hides. Jurisdiction in Leightonstone Hundred. Eudo
    has this land and the King has the jurisdiction. * Now on the
    manor 4 ploughs are in lordship on 3 hides of this land.
       26 villagers who have 6 ploughs.
       Meadow, 60 acres; underwood, 10 acres.
       2 men-at-arms have 2 hides of this land. They have 2 ploughs.
    Value of the whole of this manor before 1066 £12; now the same.

16   LAND OF SWEIN OF ESSEX

TOSELAND Hundred
1 M. In WARESLEY Robert son of Wymarc had 7 hides taxable. Land
    for 9 ploughs. Now in lordship 2 ploughs;
       17 villagers and 4 smallholders with 2 ploughs.
       Meadow, 25 acres; underwood, 16 acres.
    Value before 1066 £8; now £6.
       Thorold holds from Swein of Essex.

17   LAND OF ROGER OF IVRY

LEIGHTONSTONE Hundred
1 M. In COVINGTON Askell had 8½ hides taxable. Land for 13 ploughs.
    Now in lordship 3 ploughs on ½ carucate (hide)* of this land.
       18 villagers who have 8 ploughs.
       Meadow, 48 acres.

De hac t̄ra tene·ɴ .ıı .milites .ıı .hid̄ .7 ibi hn̄t .ıı .car̄.
T.R.E. ual .vııı .lıb̄ .m̊ .x .lıb̄ .Roger de Ẏuri h̄t de
rege.

TERRA ARNVLFI DE HESDING.

I n *VPEFORDE* .hb̄ Bului .x .hid̄ ad glđ .T̄ra .x .car̄.
de hesdinc
Nc̄ tenet Arnulf de rege .7 monachi de cluniaco
de illo. lbi nc̄ in dn̄io .v .car̄ .7 xx .uıℏ 7 vııı .bord̄
hn̄tes .v .car̄. lbi æccla 7 pbr .7 ıı .molini .ʟ .solid̄.
7 xxıııı .ac̄ p̊ti .T.R.E .7 m̊ ual .x .lıb̄.

.XIX. **TERRA EVSTACHIJ VICECOM̄** *NORMANECROS HD̄.*

I n *SALTREDE* .hb̄ Tosti .ııı .hid̄ 7 ııı .uirg̊ 7 dim̄
ad glđ .T̄ra .vııı .car̄. lbi nc̄ in dn̄io .ıı .car̄ .7 x .uıℏ
7 ıı .bord̄ cū .ıııı .car̄. lbi æccla .7 xıııı .ac̄ p̊ti .7 xxx·
ac̄ siluæ past .T.R.E .ual .c .solid̄ .m̊ .ıııı .lıb̄ .Walter
tenet de Eustachio uicecomite.

I n *CALDECOTE* .hb̄ Stric .v .hid̄ ad glđ .T̄ra .vı .car̄.
lbi nc̄ in dn̄io .ı .car̄ .7 x .uıℏ 7 ıı .bord̄ hn̄tes .ıııı .car̄.
lbi .xv .ac̄ siluæ min̄ .T.R.E .ual .ıııı .lıb̄ .m̊ .ııı .lıb̄.
Miles eustachij tenet.

I n *WASINGELEIA* .hb̄ Tori .ıı .hid̄ 7 dim̄ ad glđ .T̄ra
ıııı .car̄. lbi nc̄ .ı .car̄ in dn̄io .7 x .uıℏ 7 ı .bord̄ .hn̄t
.ı .car̄ 7 dimiđ. lbi .xıı .ac̄ p̊ti .Silua past .vıı .q̄ʒ
7 xxıııı .ptic̄ lḡ .7 ııı .q̄ʒ lat̄ .T.R.E .7 m̊ ual .ʟ .solid̄.

Ibi fuer̄ .vıı .sochi
S̄ I n Ouretune vııı .hide 7 ı .uirg̊ tre ad glđ .T̄ra .v .
car̄ 7 ııı .bou̇ .Soca regis in Normanecros .lbi Joℏs
de Eustachio h̄t .ııı .bou̇ in car̄ .7 ıx .ac̄s p̊ti .T.R.E.
ual .xʟ .sol̄ .m̊ .xx .solid̄.

2 men-at-arms hold 2 hides of this land. They have 2 ploughs.
Value before 1066 £8; now £10.
Roger of Ivry has it from the King.

18   LAND OF ARNULF OF HESDIN

[TOSELAND Hundred]

1   M. In OFFORD (CLUNY) Bului had 10 hides taxable. Land for 10 ploughs.
Now Arnulf of Hesdin holds from the King, and the monks of
Cluny from him. Now in lordship 5 ploughs;
     20 villagers and 8 smallholders who have 5 ploughs.
       A church and a priest.
     2 mills, 50s; meadow, 24 acres.
Value before 1066 and now £10.

19   LAND OF EUSTACE THE SHERIFF

206 a

NORMANCROSS Hundred

1   M. In SAWTRY Tosti had 3 hides and 3½ virgates taxable. Land
    for 8 ploughs. Now in lordship 2 ploughs;
      10 villagers and 2 smallholders with 4 ploughs. A church.
      Meadow, 14 acres; woodland pasture, 30 acres.
    Value before 1066, 100s; now £4.
    Walter holds from Eustace the Sheriff.

2   M. In CALDECOTE Stric had 5 hides taxable. Land for 6 ploughs.
    Now in lordship 1 plough;
      10 villagers and 2 smallholders who have 4 ploughs.
      Underwood, 15 acres.
    Value before 1066 £4; now £3.
    A man-at-arms of Eustace holds it.

3   M. In WASHINGLEY Thori had 2½ hides taxable. Land for 4 ploughs.
    Now in lordship 1 plough.
      10 villagers and 1 smallholder have 1½ ploughs.
      Meadow, 12 acres; woodland pasture 7 furlongs and 24
         perches long and 3 furlongs wide.
    Value before 1066 and now 50s.

4   S. In ORTON* 8 hides and 1 virgate of land taxable. Land for 5
    ploughs and 3 oxen. In the King's Jurisdiction*, in Normancross;
    there were 7 Freemen. Now John has 3 oxen in a plough and 9
    acres of meadow from Eustace.
    Value before 1066, 40s; now 20s.

§ In Sticiltone . 11 . hid 7 1 . uirg̃ træ ad glđ . Tra . 111 . car̃
7 1 . bou . Ibi Joħs ħo Euſtacħij ħt . vi . bou arantes . 7 11 .
focħ 7 11 . uiłł cũ . 1 . car̃ . Ibi . xvi . ac̃ p̃ti . 7 v ; ac̃ filue
minutæ . T.R.E . 7 m̃ uał . xl . folid .

Ꝏ In OVRETVNE . ħb Elſi ; vii : hid 7 dim ad glđ . Tra
v . car̃ . Ibi nc̃ in dñio . 1 . car̃ . 7 xii . uiłł 7 11 . borđ
cũ . 1 . car̃ 7 dimid . Ibi æccła . 7 lvii . ac̃ p̃ti . T.R.E .
uał . 1111 . liƀ . m̃ . xl . foł .

§ Ibidẽ Aluriz . 11 . hid 7 dim ad glđ ; Tra ; 11 ; car̃ . Soca
in Normanefcros . Nc̃ Roger ħo Euſtacħij ħt ibi
1111 . borđ 7 v . boues in car̃ . T.R.E . uał xx . foł . m̃ . v . foł .

Ꝏ In CESTRETVNE . ħƀr . 11 . frs . 1111 . hid 7 11 . uirg̃ træ
ad glđ . Tra . vii . car̃ . Ibi nc̃ in dñio . 11 . car̃ . 7 x . uiłł
7 11 . borđ ħñtes . 111 . car̃ . Ibi æccła 7 pƀr . 7 xx . ac̃ p̃ti .
7 1 . c̃fuetud in filuą aƀƀis de Burg reddeʃ . 11 . folid .
T.R.E . uał . 1111 . liƀ . m̃ fimilit . Duo milites teñ de Euſtacħ .

Ꞇ In Botuluefbrige . Boret 7 Turchil pƀri . ħƀr unã æccła
§ MARIE cũ . 11 . hid træ ad glđ . Tra . 11 . car̃ . Modo teñ
idem ipſi de Euſtachio . 7 ħñt ibi . 11 . car̃ . 7 111 . ac̃s p̃ti .
T.R.E . 7 m̃ uał xl . folid .

In Stiuecle   ħt Euſtachi . 1 . uirg̃ træ ad glđ . Waſta . ẽ
Herƀt tenet de eo .   KENEBALTVNE . HVND .

Ꝏ In SVINESHEFET . ħb Furſa dim hid ad glđ . Tra
dim car̃ . cũ faca 7 foca . Ibi m̃ . 1 . uiłłs 7 111 . ac̃ p̃ti .
Silua paſt . 1 . leſ lg̃ . 7 1 . q̃z lat . T.R.E . uał . xv . foł .
m̃ . vi . foł . Radulf teñ de Euſtachio .

Also in Jurisdiction*

5 S. IN STILTON 2 hides and 1 virgate of land taxable. Land for 3 ploughs
and 1 ox, John, Eustace's man, has 6 oxen ploughing;
2 Freemen; 2 villagers with 1 plough.
Meadow, 16 acres; underwood, 5 acres.
Value before 1066 and now 40s.

6 M. In ORTON* Alfsi had 7½ hides taxable. Land for 5 ploughs.
Now in lordship 1 plough;
12 villagers and 2 smallholders with 1½ ploughs. A church.
Meadow, 57 acres.
Value before 1066 £4; now 40s.

7 S. There Aelfric also had 2½ hides taxable. Land for 2 ploughs.
Jurisdiction in Normancross.
Now Roger, Eustace's man, has 4 smallholders and 5
oxen in a plough.
Value before 1066, 20s; now 5s.

8 2/M In CHESTERTON two brothers had 4 hides and 2 virgates of land
taxable. Land for 7 ploughs. Now in lordship 2 ploughs;
10 villagers and 2 smallholders who have 3 ploughs.
A church and a priest.
Meadow, 20 acres; 1 customary due in the Abbot of
Peterborough's woodland, which pays 2s.
Value before 1066 £4; now the same.
2 men-at-arms hold from Eustace.

9 T. In BOTOLPH BRIDGE the priests Burgred and Thorkell had a
church, St. Mary's, with 2 hides of land taxable. Land for 2
ploughs. They still hold it from Eustace. They have 2 ploughs
and 3 acres of meadow.
Value before 1066 and now 40s.

[HURSTINGSTONE Hundred]
10 In STUKELEY...... Eustace has 1 virgate of land taxable. Waste.
Herbert holds from him.

KIMBOLTON Hundred*
11 M. In SWINESHEAD Fursa had ½ hide taxable. Land for ½ plough, with
full jurisdiction.
Now 1 villager.
Meadow, 3 acres; woodland pasture 1 league long and 1
furlong wide.
Value before 1066, 15s; now 6s.
Ralph holds from Eustace.

Ⓜ **I**n *CATEWORDE*. h̄b Auic.iii.hid ad glđ. Tra
iiii.car. Ibi nc̄ h̄t Euſtach.ii.car.7 viii.uiłł
7 iiii.borđ h̄ntes.iiii.car.7 i.molin.ii.ſolidoʒ.
T.R.E.7 m̄ uał.lx.ſoł. De hac tra h̄t reſ ſoca 7 ſocā.

Ⓜ **I**n *HEREGRAVE*. h̄b Lancfer.i.uirg træ ad glđ.
Tra.ii.boū. Ibi nc̄ Herbt hō Euſtachij arai cū dim
car.7 h̄t.i.uiłłm.7 vi.ac̄s p̄ti.T.R.E.7 m̄.v.ſolid uał.
Toui clamat hanc trā ab Euſtach ſibi injuſte ablatā.

Ⓜ **I**BIDĒ. h̄b Aluuine.i.hid træ. Tra.i.car 7 dim.
Ibi nc̄ in dn̄io.i.car.7 vii.ac̄ p̄ti.7 ii.ac̄ ſiluæ min.
T.R.E.7 m̄ uał.xx.ſolid. Herbt 7 Edmar ten de Euſtach.

Ṡ **I**n Redinges.vi.ſochi ideſt Aluuold 7 v.frs ej
h̄br.iiii.hid 7 dim ad glđ.Tra.vi.car. SOCA in Acu
meſberie Ⓜ regis. Nc̄ h̄t Euſtachi 7 Ingelrān de eo.
Ibi nc̄.ii.car in dn̄io.7 xvi.uiłł 7 iiii.borđ cū vi.car.
Ibi xxii.ac̄ p̄ti. T.R.E.7 m̄ uał.iiii.liḃ.
Aluuold 7 frs ſui clama Euſtach ſibi injuſte abſtu
liſſe hanc trā. De hac tra calūniat Wiłts inganie
dimid uirg 7 xviii.ac̄s træ.Teſtim tot̄i hund.

Ṫ **I**n Wineuuiche h̄b Aſchil.ii.hid 7 dim ad glđ.
cū ſaca 7 ſoca. Euſtach h̄t nc̄ 7 Oilard de eo.

Ṡ **I**bidē h̄br Aluuold Leuuine 7 Eilaf.ii.hid 7 dim
ad glđ.Tra.ii.car 7 dim. SOCA in Acumeſberie
Ⓜ regis. Nc̄ h̄t Euſtach 7 Oilard de eo.7 ibi nc̄ in
dn̄io.iii.car.7 xv.uiłł h̄ntes.vi.car.7 xx.ac̄ p̄ti.
T.R.E.7 m̄ uał.iiii.liḃ.

Ṡ **I**n Torninge.v.hid ad glđ. Tra.v.car. SOCA in
acumeſberie. Ibi nc̄ in dn̄io.i.car 7 dim.7 vi.uiłł
7 i.borđ h̄nt.ii.car 7 dim. Ibi xxiiii.ac̄ p̄ti. T.R.E.

12 **M. In CATWORTH** Aefic had 3 hides taxable. Land for 4 ploughs.
   Now Eustace has 2 ploughs there; and
       8 villagers and 4 smallholders who have 4 ploughs.
       1 mill, 2s.
   Value before 1066 and now 60s.
       The King has the full jurisdiction of this land.

13 **M. In HARGRAVE** Langfer had 1 virgate of land taxable. Land for 2
   oxen. Now Herbert, Eustace's man, ploughs it with ½ plough.
   He has
       1 villager.
       Meadow, 6 acres.
   Value before 1066 and now 5s.
       Tovi claims this land from Eustace, as unjustly taken from him.

14 **M.** There also Young Alwin had 1 hide of land. Land for 1½ ploughs.
   Now in lordship 1 plough.
       Meadow, 7 acres; underwood, 2 acres.
   Value before 1066 and now 20s.
       Herbert and Edmer hold from Eustace.

15 **S. In GIDDING** 6 Freemen, that is Alfwold and his five brothers,
   had 4½ hides taxable. Land for 6 ploughs. Jurisdiction in
   the King's manor of Alconbury. Now Eustace has it, and
   Ingelrann from him. Now 2 ploughs in lordship.
       16 villagers and 4 smallholders with 6 ploughs.
       Meadow, 22 acres.
   Value before 1066 and now £4.
       Alfwold and his brothers claim that Eustace took this land from
   them unjustly. William the Artificer* claims ½ virgate and 18
   acres of this land. This is the witness of the whole Hundred.

16 **T. In WINWICK** Askell had 2½ hides taxable, with full jurisdiction.
   Eustace has it now, and Odilard* from him.

17 **S.** There also Alfwold, Leofwin and Elaf had 2¾ hides taxable.
   Land for 2½ ploughs. Jurisdiction in the King's manor of
   Alconbury. Now Eustace has it, and Odilard from him.
   Now in lordship 3 ploughs;
       15 villagers who have 6 ploughs.
       Meadow, 20 acres.
   Value before 1066 and now £4.

18 **S. In THURNING** 5 hides taxable. Land for 5 ploughs. Jurisdiction in
   Alconbury. Now in lordship 1½ ploughs.
       16 villagers and 1 smallholder have 2½ ploughs.
       Meadow, 24 acres.

7 m̃ ual . LX . fol . Alured 7 Gozelin̓ ten de Euſtacħ.

Robt̓ diſpenſator clam̓ . I . uirg̓ 7 . I . hidã.

S̓ In Lolinĉtune . II . hid 7 dim̓ ad glđ . Tra . III . car̓.

Soca in Acumeſberie . ᛗ regis . Ibi nc̃ in dñio . I . car̓.

7 I . uilł 7 VI . borđ . cũ . I . car̃ . 7 IIII . ac̃ p̃ti . T.R.E. ual

LX . fol . m̃ . XL . fol . Ingelrann̓ 7 Erluin̓ ten de Euſtacħ.

S̓ In Weſtune . I . hid ad glđ . Tra . II . car̃ . Soca in Acumeſ

berie . Ibi nc̃ in dñio dim̓ car̃ . 7 IIII . uilłi cũ dim̓ car̃.

T.R.E. 7 m̃ ual . XX . folid̓ . Gulbt̓ ten de Euſtachio.

In Ciluelai ħbr Gode 7 Vluric̓ dim̓ hid tre ad glđ.

Tra . I . car̃ . Nc̃ ħt Euſtachius.

In Grafhã ħt Euſtachi̓ dim̓ hid 7 Oilard̓ Lardar̓

de eo . 7 arat ibi cũ . VI . bob̓ . Valet . X . fol.

206 c ᛗ In EMINGEFORDE ∫TOLESLVND HVND̓.

ħb Orduui . IIII . hid ad glđ . Tra . III . car̃.

Ibi nc̃ in dñio . I . car̃ . 7 II . uilł 7 II . borđ hñtes . II . bou̓ in car̃.

Ibi . XX . ac̃ p̃ti . T.R.E. ual XL . folid̓ . m̃ XX . folid̓

In Papeuuorde . I . hida ad glđ . Tra . I . car̃ . Ibi ħt Euſtacħ

in dñio . I . car̃ . 7 X . ac̃s p̃ti . T.R.E. ual . LX . fol . m̃ XX . fol.

ᛗ In OPEFORDE . ħb Aluuin̓ . III . hid ad glđ . Tra . III.

car̃ . Ibi nc̃ . IIII . borđ cũ . II . bob̓ . 7 IIII . ac̃ p̃ti . T.R.E.

ual . XL . fol . m̃ XII . folid̓ . Odo tenet de Euſtachio

In Wedereſle . ħb Sũmerled dim̓ hiđ ad glđ . Tra

dim̓ car̃ . Waſta . c̃ . Roger̓ tenet de Euſtachio . T.R.E.

ual . X . fol . m̃ . II . folid̓.

Value before 1066 and now 60s.
  Alfred and Jocelyn hold from Eustace. Robert the Bursar
claims 1 virgate and 1 hide.

19 S. In LUDDINGTON 2½ hides taxable. Land for 3 ploughs.
  Jurisdiction in the King's manor of Alconbury. Now in
  lordship 1 plough;
    1 villager and 6 smallholders with 1 plough.
    Meadow, 4 acres.
  Value before 1066, 60s; now 40s.
    Ingelrann and Herlwin hold from Eustace.

20 S. In (OLD) WESTON *1 hide taxable. Land for 2 ploughs.
  Jurisdiction in Alconbury*. Now in lordship ½ plough.
    4 villagers with ½ plough.
  Value before 1066 and now 20s.
    Wulfbert* holds from Eustace.

21 In WOOLLEY Golde* and Wulfric had ½ hide of land taxable.
  Land for 1 plough. Now Eustace has it.

22 In GRAFHAM Eustace has ½ hide; Odilard the Larderer holds
  from him. He ploughs there with 6 oxen.
  Value 10s.

  TOSELAND Hundred   206 c
23 M. In HEMINGFORD Ordwy had 4 hides taxable. Land for 3 ploughs.
  Now in lordship 1 plough;
    2 villagers and 2 smallholders who have 2 oxen in a plough.
    Meadow, 20 acres.
  Value before 1066, 40s; now 20s.

24 M. In PAPWORTH 1 hide taxable. Land for 1 plough. Eustace has 1
  plough in lordship.
    Meadow, 10 acres.
  Value before 1066, 60s; now 20s.

25 M. In OFFORD Alwin the Sheriff had 3 hides taxable. Land for 3
  ploughs.
    Now 4 smallholders with 2 oxen.
    Meadow, 4 acres.
  Value before 1066, 40s; now 12s.
    Odo holds from Eustace.

26 In WARESLEY Summerled had ½ hide taxable. Land for ½
  plough. Waste. Roger holds from Eustace.
  Value before 1066, 10s; now 2s.

ᚻ In WESTONE . ħɓ Ælget . I . hid 7 dim ad gld̄ . Tra . I .
cař 7 dim̄ . In dn̄io . ē dimidia hida de hac tra . Ibi nc̄
IIII . uilli hn̄t . I . cař . Siluæ past . xx . ac̄s . T.R.E. ual
xL . fot . m̄ . xx . fot . Judita clamat hanc tra . fup Euſtach . comitiſſa

ᚻ Ibidē ħɓ Goduine dimid hida ad gld̄ . Tra dim cař .
Ibi ht̄ Euſtach dim cař . 7 x . ac̄s p̄ti . 7 x . ac̄s filuæ past .
T.R.E. ual x . fot . m̄ . v . fot .

ᚻ In SVTHAM . ħɓ Dunninc . IIII . hid 7 dim ad gld̄ .
Tra . VIII . cař . Ibi nc̄ in dn̄io . I . cař . in una hida
7 dimidia huj træ . 7 xīī . uilt hn̄tes . v . cař . 7 I . piſcaria
mille Anguillaru̅ . 7 īīī . pſentationes p annu̅ ualent . es
xLIX . denař . Ibi . xx . ac̄ p̄ti . 7 xLVIII . ac̄ filuæ
past . T.R.E. ual . c . fot . m̄ . Lxx . fot .

ᚻ In PIRIE . ħɓ Aluuin . I . hid ad gld̄ . Tra . II . cař . deule 9
Ibi nc̄ in dn̄io . I . cař 7 dim̄ . 7 VI . uilt cu̅ . I . cař . Ibi æcclia
7 IIII . ac̄ p̄ti . Silua past . I . lev lḡ . 7 IIII . q̄q̄ lat . T.R.E.
7 m̄ ual . xL . folid .

In Buchetone Godric pbr . I . hida ad gld̄ . Tra . II . cař . 9
Ibi nc̄ . I . cař . 7 v . uilli hn̄t dim cař . Ibi . VII . ac̄ p̄ti .
T.R.E. ual . xx . fot . m̄ . x . folid .

In CATEWORDE ħɓ Rex Edw . II . hid ad gld̄ . Tra
III . cař . Ibi fuer . VIII . taini . hn̄tes fub rege faca 7 foca .
hanc tra tenuit Euſtachi . 7 m̄ eſtt in manu regis . 9
7 ibi funt VIII . hőes . 7 fub eis VII . bord . cu̅ . III . cař .
Ibi . III . ac̄ p̄ti . T.R.E. ual . xL . fot . m̄ xxx . fot .

27 M. In (HAIL) WESTON Alfgeat had 1½ hides taxable. Land for 1½ ploughs. In lordship ½ hide of this land.
　　　Now 4 villagers have 1 plough.
　　　Woodland pasture, 20 acres.
　　Value before 1066, 40s; now 20s.
　　Countess Judith claims this land from Eustace.

28 M. There Godwin also had ½ hide taxable. Land for ½ plough.
　　Eustace has ½ plough there.
　　　Meadow, 10 acres; woodland pasture, 10 acres.
　　Value before 1066, 10s; now 5s.

29 M. In SOUTHOE Dunning had 4½ hides taxable. Land for 8 ploughs.
　　Now in lordship 1 plough on 1½ hides of this land;
　　　12 villagers who have 5 ploughs.
　　　1 fishery, 1,000 eels; 3 presentations a year, value 49d;
　　　　meadow, 20 acres; woodland pasture 48 acres.
　　Value before 1066, 100s; now 70s.

30 M. In (WEST) PERRY Alwin Devil had 1 hide taxable. Land
　　for 2 ploughs. Now in lordship 1½ ploughs;
　　　6 villagers with 1 plough. A church.
　　　Meadow, 4 acres; woodland pasture 1 league long and 4
　　　　furlongs wide.
　　Value before 1066 and now 40s.

31 　In BOUGHTON Godric the priest had 1 hide taxable. Land
　　for 2 ploughs. Now 1 plough there.
　　　5 villagers have ½ plough.
　　　Meadow, 7 acres.
　　Value before 1066, 20s; now 10s.

　　[LEIGHTONSTONE Hundred]
32 　In CATWORTH King Edward had 2 hides taxable. Land for 3
　　ploughs. There were 8 thanes who had full jurisdiction under
　　the King. Eustace held this land; now it is in the King's hands.
　　　8 men there, and under them 7 smallholders with 3 ploughs.
　　　Meadow, 3 acres.
　　Value before 1066, 40s; now 30s.

XX. TERRA JVDITÆ COMITISE *NORMANECROS HD.*

In *CONINCTVNE*. hb Turchill . ix . hid ad glđ.
Tra xv . car . In dnio funt . ii . hidæ 7 dim de hac
tra . Ibi nc . ii . car . 7 xxvi . uilt hntes . xiii . car.
Ibi æccla 7 pbr . 7 xl . ac pti . T.R.E . 7 m̊ . ual . ix . lib,
De hac tra fuer . vi . hidæ de æccla S̊ MARIE de
Torný . Turchil tenebat de abbe . 7 Karitate inde
reddebat . fed hoes de hundret nefciunt quanta.

In *SALTREDE* hb Turchil Judita comitiffa ten.
x . hid ad glđ . Tra . xv . car . In dnio funt de hac tra
ii . hidæ 7 dimidia . Ibi nc Judita . ii . car . 7 xxvii.
uilt . hntes . x . car . Ibi pbr 7 æccla . 7 xl . ac pti.
Silua paft xviii . q̊ʒ lg̊ . 7 iiii . q̊ʒ lat . T.R.E . 7 m̊
ual . x . lib.   *HERSTINGESTAN HD.*

In *STIVECLE* . hb Hunneue . iii . hid ad glđ . Tra
. xvi . car . 7 In dnio tra . ii . car exceptis pdictis hid.
Ibi nc Judita . iii . car . 7 xviii . uilt . 7 viii . borđ
cu . v . car . Ibi æccla 7 pbr . 7 xxvi . ac pti . Silua paft
ix . q̊ʒ lg̊ . 7 viii . q̊ʒ lat . T.R.E . 7 m̊ ual . xii . lib . Euftach
              KENEBALTVNE HVND.   caluniat.

In *MOLESWORDE* . hb Norman . iiii . hid ad glđ.
Tra . iiii . car . In dnio . e una hida de hac tra . Ibi nc
. i . car . 7 xv . uilti 7 ii . borđ hntes . v . car . Ibi lx . ac
pti . T.R.E . 7 m̊ ual . iiii . lib . Euftachi ten de comitiffa.

In *COTES* hb Tofti comes *TOLESLVND HVND.*
iiii . hid ad glđ . Tra . viii . car . Soca ptin ad Einul
uefberia cu omibʒ cfuetudinibʒ . Ibi ht nc Judita
xii . uiltos hntes . ii . car . 7 xx . acs pti . Pciu in Einuluesbie.
De hac tra ht Giflebt pbr . ii . hidas de comitiffa.

NORMANCROSS Hundred

1 M. In CONINGTON Thorkell had 9 hides taxable. Land for 15 ploughs.
In lordship 2½ hides of this land. Now 2 ploughs there;
26 villagers who have 13 ploughs. A church and a priest.
Meadow, 40 acres.
Value before 1066 and now £9.
6 hides of this land belonged to the Church of St. Mary of
Thorney. Thorkell held from the Abbot and paid an allowance
therefrom, but the men of the Hundred do not know how much.
Countess Judith holds it.

2 M. In SAWTRY Thorkell had 10 hides taxable. Land for 15
ploughs. In lordship 2½ hides of this land. Now Countess
Judith has 2 ploughs there;
27 villagers who have 10 ploughs. A priest and a church.
Meadow, 40 acres; woodland pasture 18 furlongs long
and 4 furlongs wide.
Value before 1066 and now £10.

HURSTINGSTONE Hundred

3 M. In STUKELEY Huneva had 3 hides taxable. Land for 16 ploughs.
In lordship land for 2 ploughs, apart from the said hides. Now
Countess Judith (has) 3 ploughs there;
18 villagers and 8 smallholders with 5 ploughs.
A church and a priest.
Meadow, 26 acres; woodland pasture 9 furlongs long
and 8 furlongs wide.
Value before 1066 and now £12.
D * Eustace claims it.

KIMBOLTON Hundred*

4 M. In MOLESWORTH Norman had 4 hides taxable. Land for 4 ploughs.
In lordship 1 hide of this land. Now 1 plough there;
15 villagers and 2 smallholders who have 5 ploughs.
Meadow, 60 acres.
Value before 1066 and now £4.
Eustace holds from the Countess.

TOSELAND Hundred

5 In COTTON Earl Tosti had 4 hides taxable. Land for 8 ploughs.
The Jurisdiction belongs to Eynesbury with all customary dues.
Now Countess Judith has 12 villagers who have 2 ploughs.
Meadow, 20 acres.
Its assessment is in Eynesbury.
Gilbert the priest has 2 hides of this land from the Countess.

7 ibi hɫ . I . caɼ . 7 VI . uiɫɫos cū . I . caɼ . 7 x̅x̅ . aćs p̄ti.

Valet . XL . foliđ.

꜒ In *EINVLVESBERIE* . ħɓ rex Edw̅ . IX . hid ad glđ.

Tra . XXVIII . caɼ . Ibi nc̄ in dn̄io . IIII . caɼ hɫ comitiſſa.

7 XXXIIII . uiɫɫ 7 VIII . borđ . hn̄tes . XXVIII . caɼ . Ibi

æccɫa 7 pɓr . 7 II . molini . XXXII . folidoᵹ . 7 LX . ać filuæ

paſt . In eađ uilla eſt qđđā ouile ſexcent 7 LXII.

ouiū . 7 LX . ać p̄ti . qđ deđ comitiſſa ad sc̄am Helenā.

Valet . LXX . folidos.

De fup̄diᶜtis . IX . hiđ tenet de comitiſſa Gisleɓt . II.

hiđas . 7 ibi hɫ in dn̄io . II . caɼ . 7 VIII . aćs p̄ti . Valet . XL . foɫ.

De eađ tra hɫ Alan dapifer ej . II . hid de ea Ibi fuᶰ

II . borđ . 7 uaɫ . X . foɫ . T.R.E . uaɫ ꜒ . xx . liɓ . m̄

dn̄ium comitiſſæ uaɫ . XIIII . liɓ . 7 XII . foɫ.

꜒ In *OPEFORDE* . ħɓ Norman . III . hid ad glđ.

Tra . VIII . caɼ . Ibi n̄c in dn̄io . I . caɼ . 7 XI . uiɫɫ . 7 IIII . borđ

hn̄tes . VI . caɼ . Ibi XVI . ać p̄ti . T.R.E . uaɫ VI . liɓ . m̄ . c . foɫ.

꜒ In *PACHSTONE* . ħɓ rex Edw̅ . XXV . hiđ ad glđ . Tra

XLI . caɼ . Ibi nc̄ in dn̄io hɫ comitiſſa . V . caɼ . 7 LX . uiɫɫ.

7 VIII . borđ . hn̄tes . XXXIIII . caɼ . Ibi æccɫa 7 pɓr.

7 III . molini . LXIIII . folid . 7 q̃t xx . ać p̄ti . Silua

paſt dim̄ leu̅ lḡ . 7 dim̄ leu̅ 7 I . q̂ᵹ laɫ . 7 alia filua

dimiđ leu̅ lḡ . 7 III . q̂ᵹ laɫ . De hac tra p̄tin ad æcclam

una hida . T.R.E . uaɫ XXIX . liɓ . 7 IIII . folid . modo

XXXIII . liɓ . 7 X . folid.

꜒ In *DODINCTVN* ħɓ Wallef . III . hid . ad glđ . Tra

III . caɼ 7 VI . boū . Ibi n̄c in dn̄io . I . caɼ . 7 VIII . uiɫɫ

7 I . borđ . cū . I . caɼ . Ibi XX.II . ać p̄ti . Silua paſt

V . q̂ᵹ lḡ . 7 IIII . q̂ᵹ laɫ . T.R.E . uaɫ . XL . foɫ . m̄ . LX . foɫ.

Alan tenet de comitiſſa.

He has 1 plough and 6 villagers with 1 plough. Meadow, 20 acres.
Value 40s.

6 M. In EYNESBURY King Edward had 9 hides taxable. Land for 28
   ploughs. Now the Countess has 4 ploughs in lordship;
     34 villagers and 8 smallholders who have 28 ploughs.
     A church and a priest.
     2 mills, 32s; woodland pasture, 60 acres.
     In the same village is a sheepfold, 662 sheep; 60 acres of
   meadow, which the Countess gave to St. Helen's (of Elstow).
   Value 70s.
     Gilbert the priest holds 2 of the above 9 hides from the
   Countess. He has 2 ploughs in lordship. Meadow, 8 acres.
   Value 40s.
     Her steward Alan has 2 hides of this land from her; 2
   smallholders. Value 10s.
Value of the manor before 1066 £20; now, the value of the
Countess' lordship, £14 12s.

7 M. In OFFORD Norman had 3 hides taxable. Land for 8 ploughs.
   Hugh holds from the Countess. Now in lordship 1 plough;   207 a
     11 villagers and 4 smallholders who have 6 ploughs.
     Meadow, 16 acres.
Value before 1066 £6; now 100s.

8 M. In PAXTON, with 3 outliers, King Edward had 25 hides taxable.
   Land for 41 ploughs. Now the Countess has 5 ploughs
   in lordship;
     3 mills, 64s; meadow, 80 acres; woodland pasture ½ league
      long and ½ league and 1 furlong wide; another woodland
      ½ league long and 3 furlongs wide.
     1 hide of this land belongs to the church.
Value before 1066 £29 4s; now £33 10s.

9 M. In DIDDINGTON Earl Waltheof had 3 hides taxable. Land for 3
   ploughs and 6 oxen. Now in lordship 1 plough;
     8 villagers and 1 smallholder with 1 plough.
     Meadow, 22 acres; woodland pasture 5 furlongs long and
      4 furlongs wide.
Value before 1066, 40s; now 60s.
     Alan holds from the Countess.

.XXI. TERRA GISLEBERTI ^{de Gand.} *TOLESLVND. HD̃*

Ⓜ In *STANTONE* . ħb̃ Vlf . XIII . hid ad gld̃ . Tra . XVIII .
caɼ . Ibi nc̃ Gisleb̃t de gand . in dñio . II . caɼ . XX.̇'̇'̇'̇'̇
uilł . 7 VIII . bord hñtes XI . caɼ . Ibi æccła 7 pb̃r .
7 q̃t XX . ac̃ p̃ti . T.R.E . uał XVII . lib̃ . m̃ . XVI . lib̃ .

.XXII. TERRA ALBERICI DE VER. [*TOLESLVND HVND*

Ⓜ In *GELINGE* . ħb̃ Aluric . V . hid ad gld̃ . Tra
VIII . caɼ . Ibi nc̃ in dñio . II . caɼ . 7 X . uilł 7 II . bord
cũ . III . caɼ . Ibi æccła 7 pb̃r . 7 XL ac̃ p̃ti . 7 V . ac̃
siluæ min . T.R.E . 7 m̃ uał . IIII . lib̃ .

Ⓜ In *EMINGEFORDE* . ħb̃ Aluric . XI . hid ad gld̃ .
Tra . VII . caɼ . Ibi nc̃ in dñio . II . caɼ . 7 XIII . uilł
7 IIII . bord . hñtes . V . caɼ . Ibi . II . molini . VI . lib̃ .
7 piſcina . VI . ſolidoꝝ . 7 L . ac̃ p̃ti . T.R.E . 7 m̃ uał
H̃ duo maneria teñ Aluric T.R.E.   [XII . lib̃ .
de abb̃e de Rameſẏ . m̃ tenet Alb̃eri de uer
de rege . 7 Radulf fili Oſmundi de eo .

.XXIII. TERRA WILLI FILIJ ANSCVLFI. [*TOLESLVND HD̃.*

Ⓜ In *WEDRESLEIE* ħb̃r Magne 7 Leue . II . hid|ad 7 dim̃
gld̃ . Tra . V . caɼ . Ibi nc̃ in dñio . II . caɼ . 7 V . uilł .
7 I . bord . hñtes . II . caɼ 7 dim . Ibi æccła 7 pb̃r . 7 XX . ac̃
p̃ti . 7 V . ac̃ siluæ min . T.R.E . uał . XL . ſot . m̃ . L . ſot .
Hoc Ⓜ teñ Rann̄ fr̃ Ilgerij de Willo filio Anſculfi .

21   LAND OF GILBERT OF GHENT

TOSELAND Hundred

1 M. In (FEN) STANTON Ulf had 13 hides taxable. Land for 18 ploughs.
   Now Gilbert of Ghent has 2 ploughs in lordship.
   24 villagers and 8 smallholders who have 11 ploughs.
       A church and a priest.
   Meadow, 80 acres.
   Value before 1066 £17; now £16.

22   LAND OF AUBREY DE VERE *

TOSELAND Hundred

1 M. In YELLING Aelfric had 5 hides taxable. Land for 8 ploughs.
   Now in lordship 2 ploughs;
       10 villagers and 2 smallholders with 3 ploughs.
           A church and a priest.
       Meadow, 40 acres; underwood, 5 acres.
   Value before 1066 and now £4.

2 M. In HEMINGFORD Aelfric had 11 hides taxable. Land for 7
   ploughs. Now in lordship 2 ploughs;
       13 villagers and 4 smallholders who have 5 ploughs.
       2 mills, £6; a fishpond, 6s; meadow, 50 acres.
   Value before 1066 and now £12.
       Aelfric held these two manors from the Abbot of Ramsey
   before 1066. Now Aubrey de Vere holds from the King,
   and Ralph son of Osmund from him.

23   LAND OF WILLIAM SON OF ANSCULF

TOSELAND Hundred

1 M. In WARESLEY Magni and Leofa had 2½ hides taxable.
   Land for 5 ploughs. Now in lordship 2 ploughs;
       5 villagers and 1 smallholder who have 2½ ploughs.
           A church and a priest.
       Meadow, 20 acres; underwood, 5 acres.
   Value before 1066, 40s; now 50s.
       Ranulf brother of Ilger holds this manor from William
   son of Ansculf.

XXII. TERRA RANNVLFI ⁊fris Ilgerij. *TOLESLVND HVND.*

Ⓜ In *EVRETVNE*. ħɓ Ingeuuar vii . hiđ ad glđ.
Tra . xviii . car . Ibi nc in đnio . ii . car . ⁊ xix . uilł
⁊ ii . borđ hntes . ix . car . Ibi pɓr ⁊ æccła . ⁊ xv . ac
pti . ⁊ xl . ac filuæ min . T.R.E. uał . x . liɓ . m̄ . vii . liɓ.
Rannulf ⁊fr Ilgerij tenet de rege.

.XXV. .II. TERRA ROBERTI FAFITON [TOLESLVND HVND.

Ⓜ In *WESTVNE*. ⁊Vluuin ħɓr Saxi . ii . hiđ ad glđ . Tra . vi . car.
Ibi nc in đnio f.Fafiton Roɓtus hꝉ . ii . car . ⁊ viii . uiłłos
cū . iii . car . ⁊ xl . acs filuæ paſt . T.R.E. uał . vi . liɓ.
m̄ . iiii . liɓ.

Ⓜ In *SVTHAM*. ħɓ Saxi . ii . hiđ ad glđ . Tra . iii . car.
Ibi nc Roɓt in đnio . i . car . ⁊ iiii . uilł cū . i . car . ⁊ x . ac
pti . ⁊ x . acs filuæ paſt . ⁊ v . acs filuæ min . T.R.E. uał
xl . foł . m̄ xx . folid.

.XXVI. TERRA WILLI INGANIA. *DELESTVNE HVND.*

Ⓜ In *REDINGES* ħɓ Britheue . iiii . hiđ ⁊ dim ad glđ.
Soca fuit in ħđ de Creſſeuuelle . Ibi nc in đnio
inganie Willelm hꝉ . ii . car . ⁊ xv . uilł ⁊ iii . borđ hntes . v .
car . ⁊ xx.ii . acs pti . T.R.E. uał . xl . foł . m̄ . iiii . liɓ.

XXVII. RADVLFI FILIJ OSMVNDI. *TOLESLVND HD.*

In *Emingeforde* ħɓ blach Aluuin . i . hiđ ad glđ . Tra
. i . car Waſta . ē . Radulf fili Ofmundi hꝉ.

24   LAND OF RANULF BROTHER OF ILGER   207 b

TOSELAND Hundred
1   M. In EVERTON Ingward had 7 hides taxable. Land for 18 ploughs.
    Now in lordship 2 ploughs;
       19 villagers and 2 smallholders who have 9 ploughs.
         A priest and a church.
       Meadow, 15 acres; underwood, 40 acres.
       Value before 1066 £10; now £7.
       Ranulf brother of Ilger holds from the King.

25   LAND OF ROBERT [SON OF]* FAFITON

T OSELAND Hundred
1   2 M. In (HAIL) WESTON Saxi and Wulfwin had 2 hides taxable. Land for 6*
    ploughs. Now in lordship Robert son of Fafiton has 2 ploughs; and
       8 villagers with 3 ploughs.
       Woodland pasture, 40 acres.
       Value before 1066 £6; now £4.

2   In SOUTHOE Saxi had 2 hides taxable. Land for 3 ploughs.
    Now Robert has 1 plough in lordship; and
       4 villagers with 1 plough.
       Meadow, 10 acres; woodland pasture, 10 acres;
         underwood, 5 acres.
       Value before 1066, 40s; now 20s.

26   LAND OF WILLIAM THE ARTIFICER*

LEIGHTONSTONE Hundred
1   M. In GIDDING Bricteva had 4½ hides taxable. The Jurisdiction was
    in the Hundred of ' CRESSWELL'*. Now William the Artificer
    has 2 ploughs in lordship; and
       15 villagers and 3 smallholders who have 5 ploughs.
       Meadow, 22 acres.
       Value before 1066, 40s; now £4.

27   LAND OF RALPH SON OF OSMUND

TOSELAND Hundred
1   In HEMINGFORD Alwin Black had 1 hide taxable. Land for 1
    plough. Waste. Ralph son of Osmund has it.

.XXVI. TERRA ROTHAIS VXORIS RICARD *TOLESLVND HVND.*

In *EINVLVESBERIE* ħb Robtus fili Wimarch

xv. hid ad glđ. Tra. xxvii. car. Ibi nc Rohais

uxor Ricardi ħt in dñio. vii. car.

Ibidē ħt S Neot de ea. iii. car in dñio.7|xix. uiłł ^{In ipſa uilla}

7 v. borđ hñtes. vii. car. Ibi. i. moliñ. xxiii. ſolidoʒ.

7 i. picariā q̃ app̄ciat cū Manerio.7 lxv.7 dim ač

p̄ti. T.R.E. uał. xx.iiii. lib. m̄ xxi. lib. p̄ter uictū

monachoʒ q̃ app̄ciat. iiii. lib.

De eađ tra tenet Wiłłs brito. ii. hid 7 i. uirg de ea.

7 ħt in dñio dimid. car.7 iii. uiłł 7 iiii. borđ cū. i. car.

Valet. xxx. ſolid.

207 c **XXIX.** **I** TERRA TAINORV REGIS.

In *WASINGELEI*. ħb Ch..elbert. ii. hid 7 dim

ad glđ. Tra. iiii. car. Idē ipſe tenet rege.7 ħt

ibi. i. car.7 x. uiłł cū. iiii. car. Ibi æccła 7 pbr.

7 xii. ač p̄ti. Silua paſt. vii. q̃ʒ lg.7 x. q̃ʒ 7 dim

lat. T.R.E.7 m̄ uał. x. ſolid. *DELESTVNE HVND.*

In Caiſſot ħb Aluuine. i. uirg træ ad glđ cū ſaca

7 ſoca. Tra. ii. bou. Jacet in bedefordſcira. ſ; glđ dat

in hunteđſcire. Idē ipſe ten nc de rege.7 ħt. ibi. i. uiłł

cū. ii. bob in car. T.R.E. uał. xvi. den. m̄ ſimilit.

In *CATEWORDE*. ħb Auic. iii. hid ad glđ. Trı. iiii.

car. Nc tenet Eric de rege.

7 idem ħt ſub rege. i. hid ad glđ. Tra. i. car. Ibi ħt

ii. uiłłos.7 vi. ačs p̄ti. T.R.E. uał. xl. ſoł. m̄ xx. ſoł.

In Brantune. Elric. i. hid 7 i. uirg træ ad gld. Tra

x. bou. Ibi. iii. borđ.7 i. caruca. Valet. xxx. ſolid

28 LAND OF ROHAIS WIFE OF RICHARD SON OF GILBERT

TOSELAND Hundred

1 M. In EYNESBURY Robert son of Wymarc had 15 hides taxable.
Land for 27 ploughs. Now Rohais wife of Richard has 7
ploughs in lordship. St. Neot's also has 3 ploughs from
her in lordship; and in the village itself
19 villagers and 5 smallholders who have 7 ploughs.
1 mill, 23s; 1 fishery, which is assessed with the manor;
meadow, 65½ acres.
Value before 1066 £24; now £21, besides the supplies
for the monks, which are assessed at £4.
William the Breton holds 2 hides and 1 virgate of this
land from her. He has ½ plough in lordship; 3 villagers
and 4 smallholders with 1 plough. Value 30s.

29   LAND OF THE KING'S THANES   207 c

[NORMANCROSS Hundred]

1 M. In WASHINGLEY Ketelbert had 2½ hides taxable. Land for 4
ploughs. He still holds from* the King and has 1 plough; and
10 villagers with 4 ploughs. A church and a priest.
Meadow, 12 acres; woodland pasture 7 furlongs long
and 10½ furlongs wide.
Value before 1066 and now 10s.

LEIGHTONSTONE Hundred*

2 In KEYSOE* Alwin had 1 virgate of land taxable, with full
jurisdiction. Land for 2 oxen. It lies in Bedfordshire but it
pays tax in Huntingdonshire. He still holds from the King,
and has 1 villager with 2 oxen in a plough.
Value before 1066, 16d; now the same.

3 M. In CATWORTH Aefic had 3 hides taxable. Land for 4 ploughs.
Eric now holds from the King. He also has 1 hide taxable,
under the King. Land for 1 plough. He has
2 villagers.
Meadow, 6 acres.
Value before 1066, 40s; now 20s.

4 In BRAMPTON Alric, 1 hide and 1 virgate of land taxable.
Land for 10 oxen.
3 smallholders; 1 plough.
Value 30s.

ᴍ) In *CILVELAI* ħƀr Golde 7 Vluric fili⁹ ej⁹ . iii . hiđ⁷
ad glđ . Ťra . vi . caƚ⁷ . Iđē ípſi hn̄t de rege . Ibi . i . caƚ⁷
in dn̄io . 7 xiiii . uiłł hn̄tes . v . caƚ⁷ . 7 xx . ac̄ p̄ti . T.R.E.
7 m̄ uaƚ . ʟx . foƚ.

In Saltrede . Aluuine dim̄ caƚ⁷ ad glđ . Ťra . vi . bou.
Nc̄ tenet uxor ej⁹ de rege . 7 ħ⁷ ibi . i . caƚ⁷ . 7 ii . ac̄s p̄ti .
T.R.E. 7 m̄ uaƚ . x . foƚid.

208 a
    Dicunt hōēs qui jurauer̄ in Huntedune . qđ
æccła Ꞩ ᴍᴀʀɪᴇ de burgo 7 ṫra quæ ad eā p̄tinet
fuit æcclæ de Tornẏ . ſed aƀƀ inuadiauit eā bur
genſiƀ⁹ . Rex Edw⁷ aut̄ dedit eā Vitali 7 Bernardo
p̄ƀris ſuis . 7 ipſi uendider̄ Hugoni camerario regis
Edw⁷ . Hugo ū uendidit eā . ii . p̄ƀris de huntedune.
7 hn̄t inde ſigillū regis . E . Euſtachi⁹ m̄ ħ⁷ eā ſine
liberatore . 7 ſine breui 7 ſine ſaiſitore.

Γ Euſtachi⁹ abſtulit p̄ uī domū Leueue . 7 dedit
Ogero de Lundonia.

Γ Teſtificant⁷ terrā Hunef 7 Gos fuiſſe
ſub manu regis Edw⁷ die qua uiuus
7 mortuus fuit . 7 eos de eo tenuiſſe non de comite.
Sed dicunt ſe audiſſe qđ rex . W . debuerit eā
dare Walleuo.

Γ De . v . hiđ de Broc̄tone dn̄t qđ ṫra ſochemanoᵶ
fuit . T.R.E. ſed iſđe rex dedit ṫrā 7 ſocā de eis
Ꞩ Benedic̄to de Rameſẏ . p̄pt⁷ unū ſeruitiū qđ
aƀƀ Aluuin⁹ fecit ei in ſaxonia . 7 poſtea ſēp eam
                        Γ habuit.

5   M. In WOOLLEY Golde and her* son Wulfric had 3 hides taxable.
Land for 6 ploughs. They still have it from the King. 1 plough
in lordship.
>14 villagers who have 5 ploughs.
>Meadow, 20 acres.

Value before 1066 and now 60s.

[NORMANCROSS Hundred]

6   In SAWTRY Alwin ½ carucate taxable. Land for 6 oxen.
Now his wife holds from the King. She has 1 plough.
>Meadow, 2 acres.

Value before 1066 and now 10s.

Blank column   207 d

D   [DECLARATIONS OF THE JŪRORS]*

1   The jurors in HUNTINGDON state that the Church of St.
Mary in the Borough and the land that belongs to it was the
Church of Thorney's; but the Abbot pledged it to the burgesses.
However, King Edward gave it to Vitalis and Bernard, his
priests; they sold it to Hugh, King Edward's Chamberlain.
But Hugh sold it to two priests of Huntingdon, for which they
have King Edward's seal. Eustace now has it without
deliverer, without writ and without installer.

2   Eustace took Leofeva's house by force and gave it to
Odger of London.

3   They testify that the land of Hunef and Gos was in King
Edward's hands at his death, and that they had held from him,
not from the Earl.* But they state that they had heard that
King William was going to give it to Waltheof.

4   Of the 5 hides at BROUGHTON, they state that they were
Freemen's land in King Edward's time, but that he gave the
lands and the jurisdiction over them to St. Benedict's of
Ramsey, because of a service which Abbot Alwin did for him
in Saxony;* and that [the Abbey] had had it ever since.

F Comitat̃ teſtificat̃ q̃d̃ t̃ra Bricmer
belchorne fuit Reuelande.T.R.E.7 p̃tinuit ad firmã.

F Terrã Aluuini p̃bri teſtant̃ fuiſſe abbis.
7 utrunq̃ fuiſſe t̃rã p̃bri 7 p̃fecti.

F Terrã Alurici de Gellinge 7 Emingeforde teſ
teſtant̃ fuiſſe S̃ Benedicti.7 eas fuiſſe c̃ceſſas Alurico
in uita ſua tali ratione. q̃d̃ poſt mortẽ ſuã debu
erant redire ad æcclãa.7 bocſtede cũ eis.Ipſe
autẽ Aluricus occiſus fuit in bello ap̃ Haſtinges.
7 abb̃ recepit t̃ras ſuas donec Alberic⁹ deſaiſiuit eũ.

F De.11.hid̃ quas Rad̃ fili⁹ Oſmundi teñ in Emin
geforde.dñt q̃d̃ una ex his erat in die.R.E.de dñio
æcclæ de Rameſÿ.7 c̃tra uoluntatẽ abb̃is tenere illũ.
De altera hida dñt q̃d̃ Godric⁹ tenuit eã de abb̃e.
Sed cũ abb̃ eet in Danemarka.Oſmund⁹ pat̃ Rad̃
rapuit eã a Sauuino Accipitrario.cui abb̃ eã dede
rat ob amorẽ regis.

F De Sũmerlede dñt q̃a tenuit t̃rã ſuã de Turulfo.
qui eã ſibi dedit.7 poſt de filijs ej⁹.ipſoſq̃ habuiſſe
ſacã 7 ſocã ſup eum.

F Dicunt t̃rã Wluuini chit de Weſtone p̃ ſe fuiſſe
maneriũ.7 non p̃tinuiſſe ad Kenebaltone.ſed tam̃
eũ fuiſſe hoem Hæroldi comitis

208 b F De una hida t̃re 7 dimidia quæ fuit Elget.
dñt hoẽs qui jurauer̃ q̃d̃ ipſe Ælget⸴de comite Toſti
cũ ſaca 7 ſoca.7 poſtea de Wallef.

5   The Country testifies that the land of Brictmer
Balehorn* was reeveland before 1066 and belonged
to the revenue.

6   They testify that the lands* of Alwin the priest
were the Abbot's; and were both the priest's lands
and the reeve's lands.

7   They testify that the lands* of Aelfric of YELLING
and HEMINGFORD were St. Benedict's; and that they
had been granted to Aelfric for his life-time on the
condition that after his death they should revert to the
church, and Boxted* with them. However Aelfric was
killed in the battle at Hastings, and the Abbot recovered
his lands, until Aubrey de Vere dispossessed him.

8   Of the 2 hides which Ralph son of Osmund holds in
HEMINGFORD, they state that one of them was in the
lordship of the Church of Ramsey in King Edward's day
and that Ralph holds it against the Abbot's will. Of the
other hide, they state that Godric held it from the Abbot,
but that when the Abbot was in Denmark, Ralph's father,
Osmund, took it by force from Saewin the Falconer, to
whom the Abbot had given it because of his regard for the
King. *

9   Cf Summerled, they state that he held his land from
Thorulf, who gave it to him, and afterwards from his
sons, and that they had full jurisdiction over him.

10   They state that the land of Young Wulfwin of
(HAIL) WESTON was a manor on its own, and did not
belong to Kimbolton; but that he was Earl Harold's
man.

11   Of the 1½ hides of land which were Alfgeat's, the jurors   208 b
state that Alfgeat held them himself from Earl Tosti, with
full jurisdiction, and afterwards from Waltheof.

Vnā hidā trǽ similit̃ tenuit Godric p̃br
de comite Wallef. T·R·E . quā nc̃ Euſtachius tenet.

Dn̄t Terrā Goduini de Weſtone nichil p̃tinu
iſſe ad Saxi anteceſſorē Faſitonis.

Teſtant hões de comitatu qd̃ rex Edw̃ dedit
Suineshefet Siuuardo comiti soccā 7 ſacā.7 ſic ha
buit Harold comes . p̃ter qd̃ geldabant in Hund.
7 in hoſtē cū eis ibant.

De tra Furſǽ fuit ſoca regis.

De una uirgata trǽ Aluuini Deule in Partenhale
ħb rex Edw̄ ſocā.

Dn̄t fuiſſe in ſoca regis hidā trǽ Wluuini quā
habebat in Cateuuorde . nec Heroldū comitē habuiſſe.

In parua Cateuuorde ħb idē Wluuine . I . hidā.
de qua rex Edw̃ ſēp habuit ſacā 7 ſocā . terrā aut̃
poterat dare cui uoluiſſet 7 uendere . Sed hões
comitiſſǽ dn̄t regē Walleuo trā dediſſe.

Comitat teſtat̃ qd̃ tcia pars dimidiǽ hidǽ quǽ
jacet in Eſtone 7 geldat in Bedefordſcire . p̃tinet
ad Spalduic Maneriū abb̃is de Elẏ.7 ſic abb̃ ha
buit.T·R·E.7 poſt aduent̃.W·regis.v.annis.
Hanc Euſtachi ui de ǽccl̃a rapuit 7 retinuit.

Keteleſtan dn̄t fuiſſe 7 ee . de firma regis Edw̃.
7 quāuis Aluric uicecomes ſediſſet in ea uilla. tam
ſēp reddebat de ea firmā regis & filij eɉ poſt eū.
donec Euſtachi accepit uicecomitatū . nec unquā
uider̃ uel audier̃ ſigillū regis . E . qd̃ eā foris miſiſſet
de firma ſua.

12   Godric the priest likewise held 1 hide of land from
Earl Waltheof before 1066. Now Eustace holds it.

13   They state that the land of Godwin of (HAIL) WESTON
did not belong to Saxi, the predecessor of Fafiton.

14   The men of the County testify that King Edward
gave SWINESHEAD to Earl Siward, with full jurisdiction,
and so Earl Harold had it; except that [its men] paid
tax in the Hundred, and went with them against the
enemy.

15   Of Fursa's land; it was in the King's jurisdiction.

16   Of Alwin Devil's 1 virgate of land at PERTENHALL,
King Edward had the jurisdiction.

17   They state that the hide of land which Young Wulfwin
had in CATWORTH was in the King's jurisdiction; Earl
Harold did not have it.

18   In LITTLE CATWORTH Wulfwin also had 1 hide of
which King Edward always had full jurisdiction; but
he could grant or sell the land to whom he would.
But the Countess' men state that the King gave the
land to Earl Waltheof.

19   The County testify that the third part of ½ hide which
lies in EASTON and pays tax in Bedfordshire belongs
to the Abbot of Ely's manor of Spaldwick.* The Abbot
had it thus before 1066 and for 5 years thereafter.
Eustace forcibly seized this land from the church and
kept it.

20   They state that KEYSTON was in King Edward's
revenue, and still is; and although Aelfric the Sheriff
settled in the village, yet he always paid the King's
revenue from it, and his sons after him, until Eustace
received the Sheriffdom; they have never seen or heard   r*
of a seal of King Edward's which put the land out of
his revenue.

Aluuold 7 frs|clamant Euſtachiũ ſibi injuſte trã
ſuã abſtuliſſe. 7 comitat negat ſe uidiſſe ſigillũ
uel ſaiſitorẽ qui eũ inde ſaiſiſſet.

Ea die qua rex. E. fuit uius 7 mortuus. fuit Gede
linge Berew in Almundeberie. in firma regis.

Comitat teſtificat Bucheſuuorde fuiſſe Bereuuich
in Pachſtone. T.R.E.

Triginta vi.|træ in Brantune quas Ricard clamat
ad foreſtã ptinere: dñt de dñica firma regis fuiſſe.
nec ad foreſtã ptinuiſſe.

Grafhã dñt ſoca regis fuiſſe 7 eſſe. nec breuẽ nec
ſaiſitorẽ uidiſſe qui liberaſſet eã Euſtachio.

De. vi. hidis in Coninctune dixer ſe audiſſe

qa jacuer oli in æccła de Torný. 7 cceſſe fuer
Turchillo tali ratione. qd poſt morte ſuã debeñ
ad æcclam redire cũ alijs. iii. hidis de ead uilla.
Hoc dixer ſe audiſſe ſed non uidiſſe. neq̃ inter

De tra Toſti de Saltrede dñt qd Eric fr ej
denominauit eã æcclæ de Rameſý poſt morte ſuã.
7 fris 7 ſororis ſuæ.

De Fletone dñt qd in die. R.E. tota jacebat
in æccła de Burg. 7 jacere debet.

De Tra Leuric dñt qd fuit in ſoca regis.
ſed Remigi eps oſtendit breuẽ regis Edw.
p quẽ Leuricũ cũ omi tra dederit in epiſco
patũ Lincoliæ cũ ſaca 7 ſoca.

208 c

21   Alfwold and his brothers claim that Eustace unjustly took away their land. The County deny that they have seen the seal, or an installer who put him in possession thereof.

22   In 1066 GIDDING was an outlier in Alconbury, in the King's revenue.

23   The County testify that BUCKWORTH was an outlier in Paxton before 1066.

24   They state that the 36 hides of land in BRAMPTON, which Richard the Artificer* claims to belong to the Forest, was of the King's household revenue, and did not belong to the Forest.

25   They state that GRAFHAM was and is a jurisdiction of the King's; they have seen neither writ nor installer who delivered it to Eustace.

26   Of the 6 hides in CONINGTON, they stated that they had heard that they formerly lay in (the lands) of the Church of Thorney, and that they had been granted to Thorkell on condition that after his death they should revert to the church. with the other 3 hides of this village. They stated that they have heard but not seen this, and were not present.

208 c

27   Of the land of Tosti of SAWTRY, they state that his brother Eric devised it to the Church of Ramsey after the death of himself, his brother and his sister.

28   Of FLETTON, they state that in King Edward's day it all lay in (the lands of) the Church of Peterborough, and ought to lie there.

29   Of Leofric's land, they state that it was in the King's jurisdiction, but that Bishop Remigius shows a writ of King Edward by which he gave Leofric, with all his land, to the Bishopric of Lincoln, with full jurisdiction.

Blank column   208 d

NOTES

The manuscript is written on leaves, or folios, of parchment (sheep-skin), measuring about 15 inches by 11 (38 by 28 cm), on both sides. On each side, or page, are two columns, making four to each folio. The folios were numbered in the 17th century, and the four columns of each are here lettered a,b,c,d, marked in the margin. The manuscript emphasises words and usually distinguishes chapters and sections by the use of red ink. Underlining, in black ink, indicates deletion.

HUNTINGDONSHIRE. In red, across the top of the page, above both columns; *'Huntedunscire'* page 203 a,b; *'Hunted'scire'* 203 c,d to 207 c,d; omitted 208.

B 2	FENMAN. 'Fenish' rather than 'from Fyn' (a Danish island), as EHR 25, 1910, 594.
B 7	QUARTERS. *'Ferlinga'* is here feminine; but masculine in B 1 above, B 9 below.
B 9	22 (32). Farley 'xxii'; MS 'xx ii', filled in later, in darker ink, leaving space for an additional 'x'. The number is divided below as 2 and 30.
B 18	CARUCATES. Written over 'hidae', which is underlined for deletion.
B 21	THIS SECTION is added with a finer pen in smaller lettering.
	PLOUGHS. Lordship ploughs are sharply contrasted with taxable hides throughout Hurstingstone Hundred (except for the King's manor of Hartford), and at Alwalton and Elton in Normancross Hundred; see also 6,19.
	ABBOT. Of Ramsey, see 6,3 and D 4.
1,2	PLOUGH; 15 VILLAGERS. Punctuation seeks to preserve the ambiguity of the Latin.
1,3	PLOUGHING OXEN. Or 'oxen ploughing'.
1,4	ORTON. Waterville; see 8,4, where the King 'had', not 'has', the jurisdiction.
1,6	LEIGHTONSTONE HUNDRED. Here and normally 'Delestune'; 'Lestone' in 2,8. The difference of letter form does not justify Farley's use of a capital 'L'.
2,1	2 OXEN. The figure ii, omitted by Farley, is faintly legible in the MS.
2,2	4 SMALLHOLDERS. In the MS the line below the figure 'v' is faint and misplaces; it probably means 'delete v, substitute iiii', if not, the correction adds 4 to 5, giving 9.
2,6	ORTON. See 19,4.
2,7	WULFWY. Not, as MS, Wulfwin; Bishop of Dorchester (-on-Thames), died 1067. Under his successor, Remigius, the see was transferred to Lincoln.
4	ELY. See Appendix to the notes.
4,1	ABBOT. More probable than 'Abbey', here and hereafter.
	LAND. 'terram', accusative. 'He has' (or 'had') is to be understood.
6,1	THE ABBOT OF RAMSEY HAD. These words are repeated, after the place name, in each of the sections 6,1 - 6,9; 6,11 - 6,16; 6,19 - 6,26.

6,3	THEIR. 'Suum' probably distinguishes the smaller fines they received.
	5 HIDES. Presumably the Freemen's hides.
6,7	ST. IVES. See EPNS 222 and xli.
	CHURCH AND PRIEST. Accusative case, following 'habent', they have, meaning the church and priest.
	K. Omitted by Farley.
6,11	THE ABBOT... See 6,1 above.
6,19	THE ABBOT...See 6,1 above.
	OF THESE...IN LORDSHIP. Added in small letters; see B21
6,21	LUNEN. Farley 'Iunen'. The initial is a badly formed L, see 9,4 below.
7,1	THE ABBOT OF THORNEY HAD. Repeated, after the place name, in 7,1 - 7.6.
7,8	WHITTLESEY. In Cambridgeshire; its mere extended into Huntingdonshire.
	THE ABBOT...AT £4. Written in one line across the whole page 205 a and 205 b.
8,3-4	ANSGERED. Called 'Anfredus de Waterville' in a 12th century text, VCH 331.
13,1	[KIMBOLTON HUNDRED]. Named only at 19,11 and 20,4, including places elsewhere listed under Leightonstone Hundred. Probably a manor of Harold's (see D 14 and D 10), for which he claimed the status of a Hundred.
14,1	VIRGATES WIDE. Either comparable with the measurement 'acres wide' occasionally used in some counties, or intending 'virg(ae)', rods, rather than 'virg(atae)'.
	EARL WILLIAM. There was no Earl or Count William in 1086. Emendation to 'King William' (VCH 348) is drastic. It is possible that the note was added after William of Warenne became Earl of Surrey in 1087/1089; or that it miscopied its original.
15,1	HIDES. Added above the line, without deletion mark under 'car(ucatas) t(er)rae'.
	AELLIC...JURISDICTION. The sentence is underlined for deletion.
17,1	HIDE. Added above the line, with deletion mark under 'car(ucata)'.
19,4	ORTON. Probably Orton Longueville (as also 2,6) since Orton Waterville was a Peterborough holding. Orton totals 30 hides.
	JURISDICTION. Either 'it is' or 'it was' may be understood.
19,5	ALSO IN JURISDICTION. Literally 'Another (place in) Jurisdiction'.
19,6	ORTON. See 19,4 above.
19,11	KIMBOLTON HUNDRED. See 13,1
19,15	ARTIFICER. 'Inganie' carries the double meaning of 'engineer' and of an ingenious, 'crafty', or tricky person.
19,16	ODILARD. See OEB 223.
19,20	(OLD) WESTON...ALCONBURY. Possibly Alconbury Weston (17 76).
	WULFBERT. See PNDB 418.
19,21	GOLDE. See 29,5 below.
20,3	D. The marginal mark is probably a 'd' with an abbreviation mark, intending one of several alternative possible words, as 'diratiocinari', to be decided, that mean 'disputed'.
20,4	KIMBOLTON HUNDRED. See 13,1
22	AUBREY DE VERE. See D 7.
25,1	6. 'vi' written over another figure, probably iii.
26	ARTIFICER. See 19,15 above.
26,1	CRESSWELL HUNDRED. Otherwise unknown.
29,1	FROM. Farley omits 'de'.
29,2	LEIGHTONSTONE HUNDRED...KEYSOE. See 13,2 and note to 13,1 above.
29,5	HER. Golde (Gode in 19,21 above) could be masculine or feminine, the joint tenure of a widow and son is more probable than of father and son.

D	[DECLARATIONS] Comparable lists of disputed lands occur in several other counties, usually with the headings *Clamores,* Claims, or *Invasiones,* Encroachments. The correspondence between Declarations and text Chapters is

D 1..B 12?	D 7..22,1-2	D 13..19,28	D 19..4,4	D 25..1,9;
D 2..B 10?	D 8..27,1; 6,17	D 14..13,3	D 20..1,7	19,22?
D 3..B 14	D 9..19,26	D 15..19,11	D 21..19,15	D 26..20,1
D 4..B 21; 6,3	D 10..25,1	D 16..2,9	D 22..1,6	D 27..19,1
D 5..	D 11..19,27	D 17..13,4?	D 23..10,1	D 28..8,1
D 6..	D 12..19,31	D 18..13,5?	D 24..1,8	D 29..2,6

D 3	EARL. Waltheof, who succeeded Tosti in 1065.
D 4	SAXONY. Germany in general; Alwin perhaps accompanied Bishop Aldred of Worcester's embassy to Cologne in 1054, to negotiate the return of Prince Edward.
D 5	BALEHORN. Brihtman Balehorn in Ramsey Cartulary 1,188; 3,38, about 1060.
D 6-7	LANDS. 'Terra(s)' rather than 'terra(m)' in view of 'eas' in D 7.
D 7	BOXTED. Probably Boxted in Essex (DB 20,37) held by an Aelfric before 1066.
D 8	ABBOT..DENMARK..REGARD FOR THE KING. Probably Abbot Aelfsi, in exile in Denmark about 1070, see Freeman *Norman Conquest* 4,748.
D 19	EASTON..SPALDWICK. See note to chapter 4.
D 20	r. Marginal letter, for 'require', Investigate, omitted by Farley.
D 24	ARTIFICER. See 19,15 above.

APPENDIX

THE ELY INQUIRY ('Inquisitio Eliensis'), on its last folio, gives the details reported in the Survey, with additional information on livestock, previous population, and area. The additional details are (4,1-5 above; *Inquisitio* DB 4,528; ed. Hamilton, p.166).

Population, in Abbot Thursten's time (1066)   *Dimensions in leagues*

	villagers	smallholders	ploughs		length	width
Colne	19	5	8		2	1
Bluntisham	20	5	7		2	1
Somersham	28	9	16		3	1
Spaldwick	42	8	(omitted)		3	2*
Catworth	8	0	8			included in Spaldwick
(Totals)	(117)	(27)	(39+)			
(1086 Total)	(112)	(27)	(44)			

Ely omits the 1086 population and ploughs of Somersham, but gives the numbers that Abbot Simon 'found', when he took office, as 13 smallholders and 20 ploughs; a figure for villagers was perhaps omitted. Thursten died in 1072, Simon in 1093.

Livestock (1086)	Cattle ('animalia')	Sheep	Pigs	Cobs ('runcini')	Bee-hives
Colne	----------	30	45	---------	------------
Bluntisham	12	60	30†(45)	---------	------------
Somersham	10	90	40	---------	------------
Spaldwick	7	120	30	1	4
(Totals)	(29)	(300)	(145)(160)	(1)	(4)

    *Spaldwick included three outliers 'Estou' (Long Stow, grid reference 10 70), 'Estune' (Easton, 14 71, see D 19), and 'Bercheham' (Barham, 13 75). It measures approximately 4½ miles north to south by 3 miles east to west.
    †Abbot Simon 'found' 30 pigs, but 'has' 45.

INDEX OF PERSONS

Familiar modern spellings are given when they exist. Unfamiliar names are usually given in an approximate late 11th century form, avoiding variants that were already obsolescent or pedantic. Spellings that mislead the modern eye are avoided where possible. Two, however, cannot be avoided; they are combined in the name 'Leofgeat,' pronounced 'Leffyet,' or 'Levyet.' The definite article is omitted before bynames, except when there is reason to suppose that they described the individual.
The chapter numbers of listed landholders are printed in italics.

INDEX OF PLACES

The name of each place is followed by (i) the initial of its Hundred and its location on the Map in this volume; (ii) its National Grid reference; (iii) chapter and section references in DB. Bracketed figures denote mention in sections dealing with a different place. Unless otherwise stated, the identifications of the English Place Names Society and the spellings of the Ordnance Survey are followed for places in England; of OEB for places abroad. A star (*) marks places outside Huntingdonshire. The National Grid reference system is explained on all Ordnance Survey maps, and in the Automobile Association Handbooks; the figures reading from left to right are given before those reading from bottom to top of the map. All places in Huntingdonshire are in the 100 kilometer grid square lettered TL. The Huntingdonshire Hundreds are Hurstingstone (H); Leightonstone (L); Normancross (N); and Toseland (T).
In a few cases it has been necessary to give the same map number to adjacent places.

Upwood	H 2	25 82	6,5	Whittlesey*	N 11	26 97	7,8
(Wood) Walton	N 26	21 80	14,1	Winwick	L 4	10 80	19,16-17
Warboys	H 4	30 80	6,11	Wistow	H 3	27 80	6,4
Waresley	T 18	24 54	16,1. 19,26. 23,1	Woodstone	N 8	18 97	7,3
Washingley	N 17	13 89	19,3. 29,1	Woolley	L 15	14 74	19,21. 29,5
(Hail) Weston	T 14	16 62	19,27-28. 25,1.	Wyton	H 13	27 72	6,9
			D 10; 13	Yaxley	N 16	17 91	7,1
(Old) Weston	L 8	09 77	6,24. 19,20	Yelling	T 12	26 62	6,15. 22,1. D 7

Places not in Huntingdonshire

In Adjoining Counties
BEDFORDSHIRE 2,9. 29,2. D 19. Indexed above, Everton; Keysoe; Pertenhall; Swineshead.
CAMBRIDGESHIRE. Crowland*, Ely*, Thorney*; indexed above, Papworth, Whittlesey.
NORTHAMPTONSHIRE 1,2. Indexed above, Hargrave, Luddington, Lutton, Peterborough*,
    Thurning
see Abbot in INDEX OF PERSONS

Elsewhere in Britain
(Dorchester-on-Thames), see Bishop. (Elstow) 20,6. Hastings D 7. Lincoln, see Bishop;
    St. Mary's. London D 2.

Outside Britain
Bolbec, see Hugh. (Brittany), see William the Breton. Cluny 18,1. Coutances, see Bishop.
    Denmark D 8. Eu, see Count of Eu. Hesdin, see Arnulf. Ivry, see Roger. Saxony, D 4.
    Ver(e), see Aubrey. Warenne, see William.

SYSTEMS OF REFERENCE TO DOMESDAY BOOK

The manuscript is divided into numbered chapters, and the chapters into sections, usually
marked by large initials and red ink. Farley however did not number the sections. References
have therefore been inexact, by folio numbers, which cannot be closer than an entire page or
column. Moreover, half a dozen different ways of referring to the same column have been
devised. In 1816 Ellis used three separate systems in his indices; (i) on pages i-cvii; 435-518;
537-570; (ii) on pages 1-144; (iii) on pages 145-433 and 519-535. Other systems have since
come into use, notably that used by Vinogradoff, here followed. This edition numbers the
sections, the normal practicable form of close reference; but since all discussion of Domesday
for three hundred years has been obliged to refer to page or column, a comparative table will
help to locate references given. The five columns below give Vinogradoff's notation, Ellis'
three systems, and that employed by Welldon Finn and others. Maitland, Stenton, Darby and
others have usually followed Ellis (i).

Vinogradoff	Ellis (i)	Ellis (ii)	Ellis (iii)	Finn
152 a	152	152 a	152	152 ai
152 b	152	152 a	152.2	152 a2
152 c	152 b	152 b	152 b	152 bi
152 d	152 b	152 b	152 b.2	152 b2

In Huntingdonshire, the relation between the Vinogradoff column notation, here followed,
and the chapters and sections is

203 a	B 1-B 14	205 a	6,26-7,8	207 a	20,7-23,1
b	B 15-B 20. L	b	8,1-9,4	b	24,1-28,2
c	1,1-1,10	c	10,1-13,4	c	29,1-29,6
d	2,1-2,9	d	13,4-18,1	d	blank column
204 a	3,1-5,2	206 a	19,1-19,11	208 a	D 1-D 10
b	6,1-6,7	b	19,12-19,23	b	D 11-D 26
c	6,7-6,16	c	19,23-19,32	c	D 26-D 29
d	6 16-6,26	d	20,1-20,7	d	blank column

TECHNICAL TERMS

Many words meaning measurements have to be transliterated. But translation may not dodge other problems by the use of obsolete or made-up words which do not exist in modern English. The translations here used are given in italics. They cannot be exact; they aim at the nearest modern equivalent. Words of uncertain or arguable meaning are marked with a star (*).

MARGINAL INITIALS. D..disputed possession (see 20,3 note). K..a claim (*klamor*, or *kalumpnia*). M..*manerium* (manor). r..*require* (investigate). S..*Soca* (jurisdiction, etc.). T..*terra* (land).

BEREWIC. An outlying place, attached to a manor. *o u t l i e r*
BORDARIUS. Cultivator of inferior status, usually with a little land. *s m a l l h o l d e r*
CARUCA. A plough, with the oxen who pulled it, usually reckoned as 8. *p l o u g h*
CARUCATA. Normally the equivalent of a *hide*, in former Danish areas. *c a r u c a t e*
CILT.* *Childe,* an honourable appellation. *Y o u n g*
COTARIUS. Inhabitant of a *cote*, cottage, often without land. *c o t t a g e r*
DOMINIUM.* The mastery or dominion of a lord (*dominus*); including ploughs, land men, villages, etc., reserved for the lord's use; often concentrated in a *home farm* or *demesne,* a 'Manor Farm' or 'Lordship Farm'. *l o r d s h i p*
FIRMA. Old English *feorm,* provisions due to the King; a fixed sum paid in place of these and of other miscellaneous dues; land owing such payment. *r e v e n u e*
GELDUM. The principal royal tax, originally levied during the Danish wars, normally at an equal number of pence on each *hide* of land. *t a x*
HIDE.* A unit of land measurement, reckoned at 120 acres, but often different in practice; a unit of tax assessment, often differing from the cultivated hides. *h i d e*
HUNDRED. A district within a shire, whose assembly of notables and village representatives usually met about once a month. *H u n d r e d*
INLAND. Old English lord's land, usually exempt from tax, comparable with *dominium*. *i n l a n d*
LEUGA. A measure of length, probably about a mile and a half. *l e a g u e*
PRAEPOSITUS, PRAEFECTUS. Old English *gerefa*, a royal officer. *r e e v e*
SACA.* German *Sache,* English *sake,* Latin *causa,* affair, lawsuit; the fullest authority normally exercised by a lord. *f u l l j u r i s d i c t i o n*
SAISITOR. Royal officer who formally installed a man in possession. *i n s t a l l e r*
SOCA.* 'Soke', from *socn,* to seek, comparable with Latin *quaestio.* Jurisdiction, with the right to receive fines and a multiplicity of other dues. District in which such *soca* is exercised; a place in a *soca.* *j u r i s d i c t i o n*
SOCMANNUS.* 'Soke man,' liable to attend the court of a *soca* and serve its lord; free from many villager's burdens; before 1066 often with more land and higher status than villagers (see, e.g., Middlesex, Appendix 1); bracketed in the Commissioners' brief with the *liber homo* (free man). *F r e e m a n*
TAINUS, TEGNUS. Person holding land from the King by special grant; in former times used of the King's chief ministers and companions. *t h a n e*
T.R.E. *tempore regis Edwardi,* in King Edward's time. *b e f o r e 1 0 6 6*
VILLA. Translating Old English *tun,* town. The later distinction between a small *village* and a large *town* was not yet in use in 1086. *v i l l a g e*
VILLANUS. Member of a *villa. v i l l a g e r*
VIRGATA. A fraction of a *hide,* usually a quarter, notional 30 acres. *v i r g a t e*

KEY TO THE MAP

Hurstingstone Hundred

1. Ramsey
2. Upwood
3. Wistow
4. Warboys
5. Abbots Ripton
6. Broughton
7. Somersham
8. Colne
9. Bluntisham
10. Stukeley
11. Huntingdon
12. Hartford
13. Wyton
14. Houghton
15. St. Ives
16. Holywell

Leightonstone Hundred

1. Luddington
2. Thurning
3. Gidding
4. Winwick
5. Hamerton
6. Coppingford
7. Upton
8. Old Weston
9. Buckworth
10. Alconbury
11. Keyston
12. Bythorn
13. Brington; Molesworth
14. Leighton Bromswold
15. Woolley
16. Catworth
17. Little Catworth
18. Spaldwick
19. Easton
20. Ellington
21. Brampton
22. Godmanchester
23. Hargrave
24. Covington
25. Grafham
26. Kimbolton
27. Swineshead
28. Pertenhall
29. Keysoe

Normancross Hundred

1. Stibbington
2. Sibson
3. Water Newton
4. Chesterton
5. Alwalton
6. Orton
7. Botolph Bridge
8. Woodstone
9. Fletton
10. Stanground
11. Whittlesey
12. Elton
13. Haddon
14. Morborne
15. Normancross
16. Yaxley
17. Washingley
18. Folkesworth
19. Stilton
20. Caldecote
21. Lutton
22. Denton
23. Glatton
24. Conington
25. Sawtry
26. Wood Walton

Toseland Hundred

1. Hemingford
2. Fen Stanton
3. West Perry
4. Buckden
5. Offord
6. Great Staughton
7. Dillington
8. Diddington
9. Southoe; Boughton
10. Paxton
11. Cotton
12. Yelling
13. Papworth
14. Hail Weston
15. St. Neots
16. Eynesbury
17. Gransden
18. Waresley
19. Everton

Peterborough is represented by an open circle.

National Grid figures, in square TL, are shown in the map border.

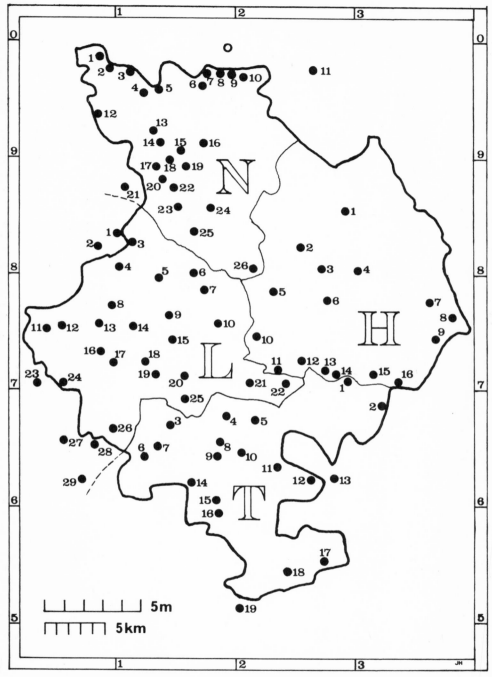

Each four-figure grid square represents one square kilometer, or
247 acres, approximately 2 hides, at 120 acres to the hide.

On the scale of this map, each dot is equivalent to about 100 acres.